D1316661

"Surrender to mystery can le̱ ...., which in turn can lead to joy and even transcendent ecstasy. The realization that there is no explanation for existence or awareness of existence is ultimate liberation. John Astin's book offers an opportunity for this liberation, if you are ready."

—**Deepak Chopra,** coauthor of *You Are the Universe*

"John Astin is a gift. He points our awareness to insights that could take a lifetime of practice to reach, but can also be apprehended by just the slightest turn of attention. With his rare blend of experience as a seasoned academic, scientist, mystic, poet, and musician, John's ability to illuminate a path toward realization with a lack of jargon and an elegant economy of words is unparalleled. This book is like walking into uncharted terrain with the kindest of guides pointing out the sublime in every step."

—**Cassandra Vieten, PhD,** president of the Institute of
Noetic Sciences

"With its miniessays and friendly practices, John's book examines experience with a vast, nondogmatic openness."

—**Greg Goode,** author of *The Direct Path* and *After Awareness*

"In his latest book, John Astin offers us a multitude of simple, straightforward, yet elegant practices for welcoming and embracing each moment of life. If you wish to discover methods of inquiry that easily peel away misperceptions of thinking, and which lead to the discovery of a lasting happiness and well-being in the midst of daily circumstances, then this is a book that deserves to be on your reading table for years to come."

—**Richard Miller,** author of *iRest Meditation* and *The iRest
Program for Healing PTSD*

"*This Extraordinary Moment* is a remarkable book that weaves together years of scholarly investigation and contemplative practice to help us understand the nature of reality. John Astin reminds us that the whole point of spiritual inquiry is to discover the ways in which our fantasies, hopes, beliefs, and ideas could never possibly capture the inconceivable depth and richness of our moment-to-moment experience. This book has the power to transform individual and collective lives."

—**Shauna Shapiro**, professor at Santa Clara University,
and coauthor of *The Art and Science of Mindfulness*

"I've never read a book that goes so deeply into the question, 'What is experience actually made of?' John Astin has created a masterpiece here that draws us into this question in a very thorough and meticulous way. If you take this book deeply, you can begin to see that he is pointing to the fact that concepts cannot pin reality down and that reality is an ever-changing flow of experience that cannot be grasped. This can be the start of a profound recognition of freedom. Highly recommended!"

—**Scott Kiloby**, author of *Natural Rest for Addiction* and
The Unfindable Inquiry

"John has taken on an impossible task—to communicate the incommunicable, to share the unshareable—yet he has written a remarkably accessible, multipronged invitation to the reader to explore their normalcy, and possibly discover for themselves the unrecognized goal of all their aspirations, unsuspectedly hidden in plain sight in the very nature of that 'normalcy.' A lucid, intelligent, and wide-ranging exploration."

—**Peter Brown**, author of *Dirty Enlightenment*

"'Live in not knowing' is a pointer you hear repeated across non-dual traditions and teachers. In *This Extraordinary Moment*, John expands this simple pointer into a complete path to awakening. Using a mixture of original metaphors, contemporary cognitive science, inquiry work, and vibrantly alive writing, the book continually invites us beyond the narrow confines of our conceptual mind into the vastness of our real experience. Highly recommended!"

—**Chris McKenna**, guiding teacher at Mindful Schools

"This wonderful, clear book invites us to drop out of metaphysical speculation and belief, stop our desperate efforts to grasp reality conceptually, and instead tune in to the direct immediacy of present (sensory, energetic) experiencing, just as it is. John offers a simple but immensely rich and subtle exploration of actual experience, revealing the depth of this extraordinary moment that is ever-changing but always here-now. Instead of turning to outside authorities, he suggests listening to experience itself. Instead of urgency and seriousness, he invites approaching this practice in a lighthearted, playful way. Nothing is an obstacle or a problem in this approach. John suggests that 'the subtlest depths are not found behind, below, or beneath but smack dab in the middle of the so-called gross or surface level of things.' This book points you to the vibrant aliveness that is right here in every moment, to be discovered not by transcending what seems ordinary and mundane, but by opening fully to the (sensory, energetic, experiential) actuality of this very moment, however it seems to be."

—**Joan Tollifson**, author of *Nothing to Grasp* and *Awake in the Heartland*

"*This Extraordinary Moment* delivers clear, engaging, refreshing, and transformational spiritual teaching. John guides the reader to awaken to the unconditional freedom and well-being that is available in every moment. This book is a must-read for anyone interested in psychospiritual evolution."

—**Jessica Graham**, spiritual teacher, and author of *Good Sex*

this extraordinary moment

MOVING BEYOND *the* MIND *to* EMBRACE *the* MIRACLE *of* WHAT IS

JOHN ASTIN, PhD

NON-DUALITY PRESS
An Imprint of New Harbinger Publications

Publisher's Note

This publication is designed to provide accurate and authoritative information in regard to the subject matter covered. It is sold with the understanding that the publisher is not engaged in rendering psychological, financial, legal, or other professional services. If expert assistance or counseling is needed, the services of a competent professional should be sought.

Distributed in Canada by Raincoast Books

Copyright © 2018 by John Astin
        Non-Duality Press
        An imprint of New Harbinger Publications, Inc.
        5674 Shattuck Avenue
        Oakland, CA 94609
        www.newharbinger.com

Cover design by Amy Shoup

Acquired by Jennye Garibaldi

Edited by Melanie Bell

All Rights Reserved

Library of Congress Cataloging-in-Publication Data on file

20   19   18

10   9   8   7   6   5   4   3   2   1   First Printing

To see a World in a Grain of Sand

And a Heaven in a Wild Flower,

Hold Infinity in the palm of your hand

And Eternity in an hour.

—William Blake

There are more things

in heaven and earth, Horatio,

Than are dreamt of

in your philosophy.

—Shakespeare

Contents

Foreword

by Adyashanti

Unless we are very careful, and very curious, we may end up living our lives lost in a world of abstraction, a waking dream that seems completely real only because it is based upon a kind of consensus delusion. For all of the amazing wonders of invention and creativity that our ability to think in abstract terms confers upon us, we can also forget that our thoughts are but representations of things and experiences. Thoughts can be useful tools of investigation and expression, but they are not ultimately real in and of themselves. As the old saying goes, the thought is not the thing...

This tool of discursive thought is so amazing and useful that we forget that the world of ideas and descriptions is not ultimately real. The thought "water" will not quench your thirst, nor will the thought "love" kiss you on the cheek or hold you in its arms. We use our ability to conceptualize for all manner of reasons, but are far more often used by it. Proof in point is the endless narrative running in our heads that we take to be real. But how can it be real? At best it's a representation of reality, but more often than not, it's nothing but a conditioned generator of alternative realities, a fiction that only exists in our minds—a sort of waking dream.

In an ever-shifting world of abstractions, we are in need of direct connection with the essence of life, as it appears moment to moment. If we are to refind our humanity, our connection, our essence, it must start exactly where we are, with the ground underfoot and the sky overhead, and our direct and immediate experience of being. It's possible to awaken from the world of our endless and conditioned inner narratives and reconnect with the immediate and wordless experience of being, pausing the button on our waking dream to breathe in the fresh air of this unfathomable existence.

This Extraordinary Moment is not only a good title for a book, it is an invitation into a profound experience of being that is, quite literally, unimaginable. It is a way of perceiving that is direct, immediate, and rich with wonder. What John has written here is really a guidebook for breaking the spell of conditioned thinking and the distorted perceptions that it creates. Its aim is to wake us up from the dream of our conditioned thinking and perceiving, to what lies on the other side of our imagination, to reality beyond words and an experience of being that is beyond the known. Read this book, but even more, contemplate it. And perhaps it will evoke within you something greater than can be imagined.

Preface

For the past two decades, I have been exploring, writing, and teaching about many of the themes found here in the pages of *This Extraordinary Moment*.

In my first book, *Too Intimate for Words* (2005), I investigated the nature of the "self" and how it is not fundamentally distinct or separate from the whole of reality. My second book, *This Is Always Enough* (2008), explored the ways in which what we are searching for is already present, that every momentary perception, every experience, is full and complete beyond measure. Finally, in *Searching for Rain in a Monsoon* (2013), I invited the reader into an experiential investigation of awareness as the ever-present, naturally open ground and basis of every moment.

A theme running throughout all of these books, however, was this growing recognition that no matter how I might attempt to frame or artic-ulate or model the nature of moment-to-moment experience, it was simply not possible to pull it off. It became clearer and clearer that by its very nature, experience radically transcended any and all efforts I might make to put it into some coherent conceptual or linguistic framework.

A couple of years after the publication of my last book, a student of mine told me about a teacher he'd been studying with, Peter Brown, who he said my own sharing reminded him of. I'd never come across Peter's work before but began to investigate it and found him to be one of the clearest, most compelling voices I'd come across in a long time. My ongoing encounter with Peter's beautifully lucid articulation of the inconceivable nature of reality continues to deepen my own understanding of this same truth. Here is a quote from him that encapsulates what *This Extraordinary Moment* is fundamentally about:

> Let go of all descriptions, and then what is this?
> You cannot say… but it is not nothing,
> and is wonderful beyond imagination.

Introduction

I teach a graduate course at Santa Clara University titled "Evidence-Based Approaches to Therapy." In the class, we explore a number of psychological therapies and review the scientific evidence concerning their effectiveness. Many of the students are struck by how unimpressive the results actually are: even those approaches which have been deemed "most effective" actually benefit only about a third of the clients, and many of them appear to have been helped only marginally. Given this modest evidence, at the end of class I pose a provocative question to my students:

"Why do you think this might be? Why, after a century of scientific psychology, have we more or less failed to identify consistently effective and lasting means to support people to flourish psychologically? Are we missing something?"

After the students spend some time discussing and reflecting on these questions amongst themselves, I drop the following bomb on them:

"Could it be that our failure to find truly effective means to liberate human beings from challenging states of mind stems from the fact that we don't actually know what those states are?"

The students look at me somewhat dumbfounded. "What do you mean we don't know what our own mental-emotional states are?" they understandably ask.

"Well," I say, "let's take one of the more common experiences that people struggle with, anxiety. Clients come to therapists, coaches, doctors, healers, and spiritual teachers because they want to feel less anxious, and teachers and practitioners suggest all manner of strategies to help them manage their anxious states of mind more effectively. Yet underlying this whole scenario are two key assumptions: first, that we actually know what this thing called "anxiety" is, and second, that so-called negative states such as anxiety are problems that must be solved. Could it be that these states we've imagined for millennia to be problems in need of solutions aren't what we have imagined them to be?"

If we wish to investigate what some material object, say a piece of metal, consists of, through inquiring into its nature we can determine that rather than being merely a "piece of metal," it is instead composed of various molecules arrayed in a particular way which in turn consist of all manner of atoms, subatomic particles, quantum fields, and so on. This book invites a similar investigation into our own subjectivity by asking a fundamental question: What are experiences *made* of, beyond the conventional descriptions and mental interpretations we bring to them?

Through a series of brief essays, explorations, and guided meditations, I invite you to investigate this question firsthand, peering around the edges of what you think your experiences are, particularly those conventionally labeled as problems (anxiety, fear, insecurity, depression, confusion), and exploring what your own experiential moments are actually composed of. As a complement to this process, there is also a host of materials available for download at the website for this book: http://www.newharbinger.com /41818. (See the very back of this book for more details.)

Through this inquiry, you may find that *all* experiences, from the most painful to the most sublime, transcend any and all attempts at mapping or modeling them. Far beyond what language and conceptualization would have us believe, *every* experience, no matter its conventional descriptive label, turns out to be ultimately unfathomable and inconceivably rich. Happiness, sorrow, pleasure, pain, joy, anger, jealousy, gratitude—no matter how we might categorize or define them, every experience is an utter free fall into endless openness, subtlety, nuance, lusciousness, and depth.

I invite you to enter into and enjoy this inquiry.

Suggestions for How to Approach This Book

One way to approach a book like this is with the hope that by engaging with its material, you will find some resolution of whatever personal issues you find yourself facing. Along with this focus on solving one's personal problems, there is often the accompanying belief or at least hope that the methods and ideas will somehow also help address the myriad social ills we see in the world today.

It's of course quite understandable that one would come to a book such as this from within this familiar human frame of reference. However, the problem with approaching it in this way is that the starting point for orienting to *any* experience as if it were a problem is the presumption that we actually know and are able to define what that experience is.

For example, let's say you're experiencing insecurity in your life and are wanting to find a way to overcome and be free of that state of mind. But, seeing insecurity as an issue that must be healed presumes that you actually know what "insecurity" is; otherwise how would you even know it was something that needed to be overcome? It is this very assumption—that we know what experiences actually are—that the inquiries in this book invite us to question.

And so, I encourage you to approach these writings more in the spirit of lighthearted, playful curiosity, not in order to fix whatever experiences or circumstances you imagine are broken about you or the world but instead to simply find out what these supposedly problematic experiential, circumstantial phenomena *actually consist of*. I invite you to approach this investigation into the nature of experience with no presuppositions about *anything* you might encounter in this inquiry. The conventional notion of being a person dealing with certain problems that must be resolved is one such assumption. Instead, just start with what's *actually* present, prior to any abstractions about its apparent implications—what it is, what it might mean about you, what it might say about life, or anything else. Start right here with whatever's appearing, simply *feeling* the presence of it, seeing how it is, how it moves, how it appears, how it vanishes. Be curious, as a child might be, about whatever is presenting itself, exploring the countless never-before-seen wonders we encounter each moment of life.

By investigating the immediacy of experience in this way, you can discover a liberating truth: in order for something even to exist as a problem that requires some solution, you must first be able to define it as an actual problem in the first place, something that turns out not to be possible owing to the ultimately indefinable, inconceivable nature of all experience.

Two Approaches to Happiness

There are, we could say, two basic approaches to manifesting a happier, more fulfilled life.

The first and most familiar to us is to try to maximize the quality of our day-to-day experiences and circumstances as best we can. This involves such things as engaging in activities and work we find fulfilling, cultivating healthy relationships with others, increasing positive states of mind, and improving our physical health and appearance. We could call all of this *learning to live life artfully or skillfully*. If you liken life to a dream, this first approach can be thought of as learning to dream the best dream possible— the most enjoyable, most fulfilling, most exciting, most enriching dream you can envision, based on what you most value.

But there is another approach to happiness and fulfillment and that is to investigate what the dream is actually made of, rather than reflexively trying to create a more desirable one. Whether we call it a happy one, a sad one, an exhilarating one, or a terrifying one, in this second approach, we simply inquire into the nature of the dreaming itself, and through this, discover that no matter its content, no matter what the dream may look like, it is *all* life, *all* reality, appearing in the many guises life can appear.

It's important to understand that this second approach doesn't preclude engaging the first and trying to create the happiest, most fulfilling life in as skillful a way as possible. However, one of the inherent challenges of trying to engineer or control our experiences and circumstances so as to maximize well-being is this: Life is invariably filled with all manner of experiences and circumstances we find difficult, challenging, or unpleasant and many of these are not very amenable (if at all) to control or change. Whether internally (thoughts, feelings, sensations) or externally (situations and circumstances), things often don't go the way we would like them to go, despite our best, most artful and sincere efforts. In other words, when it comes to manifesting the best possible waking dream, there appear to be significant limits. Which brings us back to approach two...

In an actual sleeping dream, we imagine that what's happening in the dream is in fact happening. Whether we're dreaming of having sex with a gorgeous man or woman or being chased by a monster, it all seems quite real to us until we wake up and realize it was all made of consciousness, the lover and the monster both conjured into existence by the dreaming mind.

We don't exactly know *how* consciousness is able to generate the nighttime dreams that it does, but it clearly has this extraordinary capacity. And that imagined dream world surely does seem real, at least while we're dreaming it! But could it be that our waking lives are not as different from the dream world as we imagine? Just as we can wake up and realize that the anxiety and fear experienced in the dream state is made of dream stuff, we can also "wake up" right in the midst of our everyday lives by inquiring into what the experiences we imagine we are stuck in or otherwise struggling with are actually made of. While we've evolved this extraordinary capacity to interpret, categorize, parse, and define things, careful investigation reveals that our moment-to-moment experience is not actually definable.

We imagine that we know what experiences are because we have names for them. However, through more carefully exploring the texture or felt sense of experience, we can discover that *all* experiences, whether they're conceived of as mundane or sublime, lie beyond the reach of our conceptualizing faculties. Feel into any state—fear, anxiety, joy, exhilaration—and what becomes apparent is the inadequacy of our descriptive labels, the failure of our conceptual maps to convey the unthinkably vast, subtle, and nuanced territory of experience.

So what does all of this have to do with our search for well-being? Approach one—learning to live life as skillfully and artfully as we can—is based on things actually being what we imagine them to be according to our definitions and interpretations. From this perspective, we would of course prefer to experience more of the mental, emotional, circumstantial moments we conventionally label as "positive" and have fewer of those we define as "negative."

But remember, things aren't merely what our descriptions tell us they are. They are much more than the labels we give them. And this is the liberating thing we come to realize through approach two, the discovery that those experiences conventionally labeled as happy/unhappy and fulfilling/unfulfilling are actually expressions of an ultimately indefinable, unfathomable mystery.

We can certainly try to manifest more of what we conventionally think of as "states of well-being." But the second approach reveals another order of well-being altogether, one that is discovered to be present in *every* moment of experience, irrespective of the conventional labels we may give it, a well-being that is just as present in sadness as it is in joy. This is a stable, indestructible well-being that can neither be given *nor* taken away because it is reality itself, the same ever-present reality that appears as each changing moment of life, a field of fathomless mystery and well-being that is beyond our capacity to definitively label or describe.

How to realize this? By becoming curious about our experience, exploring the unanswerable question of what experiences are made of, feeling and tasting the inconceivability of it all, waking up to the astonishing fact that experiences can never be adequately conveyed or captured by any of our descriptions or interpretations. It's fine, of course, to continue trying to live life as skillfully as you can, minimizing those states of mind and circumstances conventionally thought of as undesirable while maximizing those considered (based on your descriptions) to be more desirous. But while you engage in this more conventional approach to well-being, you can at the same time take up the second approach and begin to discover that the very experiences you've imagined yourself stuck in or troubled by are in fact infinity itself, the inconceivable, miraculous display of reality, shining forth as each instant of life, no matter its conventional label.

The Impressionistic Nature
of Experience

You've undoubtedly seen some of those remarkably beautiful Impressionist paintings. From a certain distance, one sees what appear to be discrete objects, like the floating water lilies found in several of Monet's paintings. However, the closer one gets to such paintings, the more those seemingly clear and coherent images and forms (water, flowers) reveal themselves to be patternless and incoherent points of color and light.

We find a parallel in the world of science. When the physicist examines the world, it appears at first glance to be a solid, material realm but turns out upon closer examination to be far more indefinite, ambiguous, and immaterial than was initially thought.

In much the same way that a scientist might examine the nature of molecules, atoms, and subatomic particles, we can look at our own subjective experience to see what it is "made of." Human experiences that appear quite coherent and structured from one perspective, upon closer examination, disappear into greater and greater ambiguity and incoherence.

When investigated closely, every detailed part, every aspect and tangible dimension that makes up a given experience reveals a seemingly endless array of subtler and subtler wavelike aspects, dimensions, and parts. It's an interesting paradox, isn't it, that the closer we look at the world of experience, the less clear, fixed, or definite it becomes? Just as Monet's water lilies are revealed to be points of color and light, by exploring the nature, structure, texture, and form of your present experience, you will find that it too dissolves into a vast, structureless field of vibrancy, a subtle dance of information and energy.

Ironically, even though our lives are made up entirely of experiences (what else is there, really?), rarely do we ever ask what would seem the most basic and fundamental question: "What are experiences actually made of, *experientially?*" We've tended to take it for granted that we know what things are. But like the Impressionist paintings, things aren't always as they appear. This is my invitation: to take another, closer look at the experiential painting you call your life. You may be surprised at what you find!

The Misinterpretation of Experience

Our tendency is to view certain experiences such as fear, anxiety, worry, insecurity, and confusion as problematic and then set about to overcome, avoid, heal, transcend, or otherwise improve upon them. However, there's another choice. As we've been exploring, in any moment, we can simply look and see what these supposedly negative states of mind consist of, beyond the oversimplified versions of them provided by language. For despite the myriad words we've evolved to describe what's happening experientially, we cannot actually say what anything is, at least not definitively. Try out the following practice to experience this for yourself. You can listen to a recording of it at http://www.newharbinger.com/41818.

PRACTICE

As an example, try to capture in words or concepts what is being felt and experienced right now and see if that's even possible.

You might say, "Well, this is a thought," or "that's a feeling or a sensation." But when you call something a thought, a feeling, or a sensation, what exactly are you saying? What is the experiential reality those words are pointing to?

You might answer, "Well, thoughts and sensations are ultimately made up of energy or consciousness." But this begs the question: "What in turn are the phenomena referred to as energy and consciousness made of, beyond the dictionary definitions used to describe them?"

As you investigate your experience in this way, something quite remarkable becomes apparent—every phenomenon that's encountered, no matter how it might be conventionally labeled or described, turns out to be far more than we may have imagined it to be.

Check it out for yourself. Take any descriptive label you might use… let's say it's the word "energy" or maybe "consciousness." Just feel whatever it is those words are referring to experientially. What is actually present that you describe as energy? What does the experience you call "consciousness" consist of?

As you look in this way, you'll begin to notice something extraordinary—every experience, when investigated this way, opens up to reveal more and more of itself and its nature. Feel into any experience and what's discovered is that there's so much more there—more texture, more subtlety, more depth, more mystery. As you continue exploring in this way, delving further and further into the nature and texture of experience, notice how this "moreness" that was revealed just continues to open up into even more and that it does so endlessly...

In life, we often feel as if we're somehow stuck in or confused by some experience or circumstance and then proceed to try to free ourselves from this supposed bondage and confusion. But what we call "being stuck or confused" is literally defined into existence because, when investigated, the conceptual categories of "stuck" and "confused" are seen to be neither stuck nor confused, but a swirling dance of miraculous, wide-open, inconceivable depth, intelligence, and energy.

And if such experiences are as radically open-ended and ultimately indefinable as they are, how can they possibly bind or limit us in the ways we've imagined? To put it bluntly, we suffer psychologically, not because we have certain experiences, but because of what we imagine those experiences to be through the miraculous interpretive power of concepts and language.

So, the next time you find yourself faced with something difficult or uncomfortable—a sense of lack, a feeling of confusion, a moment of upset—instead of reflexively trying to flee from or transform that state, simply inquire into or, better yet, *feel* what it is made of experientially.

There's really no answer to that question, which turns out to be the most profound of answers!

Cognitive Fusion

"Cognitive fusion," an emerging construct in psychology, refers to the belief that our thoughts about whatever is being experienced are essentially equivalent to that experience. For example, let's say I have a friend named Dave. To the extent I am fused with my thoughts about him, I will imagine Dave is who I think he is and in so doing, fail to appreciate that my thoughts about him are just that, thoughts. In short, through the mechanism of cognitive fusion, I will end up mistaking my mental interpretations of Dave for Dave himself. Practically speaking, I'll relate to my friend not as he actually is, but based on who I *imagine* him to be according to my mental caricature of him.

When we are cognitively fused (which we tend to be a great deal of the time without even realizing it), we fail to recognize that there are two distinct experiential realms:

1. the actuality of whatever person, place, or thing is being experienced and

2. our conceptualization or interpretation of that actuality.

Cognitive defusion entails recognizing that our thoughts about whatever is happening are not the same as the experience itself because those thoughts represent a gross oversimplification of whatever is occurring experientially, just as my ideas about a person like Dave (or anyone else, including myself) could never capture that person's complex, multidimensional nature.

Dave is a vast ocean of qualities and characteristics and the notion that my ideas about him accurately represent the entirety of Dave is tantamount to taking a thimbleful of water and imagining I've somehow captured the whole of the sea. The actuality of experience and our ideas about that experience can clearly coexist with neither impinging on the other. But the important thing to realize is that they are not one and the same thing any more than our ideas about what a sunrise is are somehow equivalent to the actuality of color and light dancing in the morning sky.

In many traditions, we are told that our problem is one of a lack of focus. To remedy this, we are given various meditative practices to develop greater mental focus, thereby countering the mind's tendency to become dispersed or distracted. However, what I'm suggesting here is in many respects the complete opposite. The problem of cognitive fusion is not one of too little focus but actually one rooted in *excessive* focus. For example, in any moment you find yourself seemingly caught up in some torrent of thinking or worrying, there are untold numbers of other phenomena occurring—flickers of energy, washes of sound, sparkles of color and light, all of which have absolutely nothing to do with those mental narratives.

And so, one of the keys to freeing yourself from cognitive fusion is to see that the narratives and interpretations about what is happening are infinitesimally small compared to the vastness of experience itself. By feeling the ways in which direct experience is inconceivably subtler, more complex and multidimensional than your ideas about it, you begin to uncover a profound depth and richness in everything that is encountered.

PRACTICE

Imagine for a moment a vast underwater world that stretches out before you as far as the eye can see, a world filled with unthinkable beauty and diversity—thousands of exotic creatures large and small, psychedelically colorful fish and coral, magnificent formations of rock and sand, a phantasmagoric display of life everywhere you turn…

Now imagine that your gaze suddenly falls upon one little corner of this underwater scene. You spot a tiny yellow fish swimming around in this vast oceanic world and become captivated by the fish, your attention drawn into the orbit of this colorful little creature, like a moth to a flame. You begin following the little yellow fish around. And as you do so, the rest of this scene you've been beholding begins to fade from view. Eventually, your sense of the reality of this vast underwater world is seemingly reduced to the little yellow fish.

Our everyday experience is very much like this underwater world—an infinite array of sights, sounds, textures, colors, images, and feelings filling every instant. So rich, so colorful, so deep… Presented with the vast, underwater world that constitutes our moment-to-moment experience, we invariably try to make sense of it all. We interpret it, map it, model it, conceive of it, describe it. And while all of this is completely normal and natural, the problem is that we become cognitively fused, believing our interpretations of the vast, mysterious, unfathomable world of experience are somehow equivalent to it.

It's completely understandable that we would latch onto and believe in our conceptual rendering of things, given that these interpretive frameworks bring us some measure of comfort and security, a feeling of greater certainty, a sense that we have a handle on what's going on here, how it works, and what it all means.

But just as we found ourselves doing with the little yellow fish, we become captivated and ultimately blinded by the interpretations, taken in by the narratives that claim to know what reality is. We become transfixed by the bright light of our descriptions of things, orienting so powerfully to them that we temporarily lose sight of the rest of the scene, forgetting that the interpretations are but one tiny part of an ocean of experience that is simply too vast, complex, and richly detailed to be captured by any definition or mental schema.

Bear in mind that the little yellow fish of our interpretations needn't go away; after all, such "creatures" are part and parcel of the vast and beautiful underwater world that constitutes experience. But what we *can* begin to do is feel whatever is here, sensing what is actually present, the exceedingly subtle, rich, and fathomless watery depths of experience that lie beyond the reach of anything we could ever define or conceive.

The Map Is Not the Territory

One way to understand the function of human thought is to see it as a way the organism tries to model reality. Our mental representations give us the sense that things have a kind of solidity and stability, thereby allowing us to seemingly make sense of them. Thinking is essentially an interpretive process, a natural functioning of consciousness in which mental frameworks are spontaneously generated in an effort to map the territory of experience. For example, the many ideas I might construct about who you are essentially function as a kind of map that I can use to make sense of you. But just as I might use a map of Paris to navigate around the actual city, maps, no matter how useful or detailed, can never fully capture or convey the richness and complexity of the terrains they seek to describe.

Thoughts, whether about people, places, or things, are very much like maps. What I imagine or conceive about you, however accurate that may be, is not the same as what you actually are; what I think or say a given experience is—that's happiness, that's fear, that's a tree, that's loneliness—is never the same as its incomprehensibly rich and complex nature.

In and of itself, the fact that we are conceptually and linguistically rendering experience is not the problem. However, what creates the lion's share of unrest and suffering we experience is mistaking our interpretations and resulting definitions of reality *for* reality. In short, we believe the interpretations accurately portray things, imagining our ideas about experience actually represent it when in truth, those ideas are merely ideas, approximations, or conceptual oversimplifications of something that simply cannot be reduced or collapsed into any interpretive map, no matter how seemingly accurate, elegant, or true it might be.

So, there is the reality of direct experience and then there are the conceptual frameworks and mental maps we bring to it. And that right there is the investigation I am inviting you to take up—to appreciate that the actuality of experience is distinct from its conceptual rendering and in so doing, cease confusing the two. Of course, there's nothing wrong with generating interpretations. It's what our perceiving intelligence appears to do quite naturally. But that same intelligence can also recognize, through inquiring directly into the nature of experiencing itself, that while the frameworks are able to approximate reality, they are never able to adequately capture its vastness, complexity, subtlety, and depth.

As you look into this, you may find that your interpretations deviate not just somewhat but completely from the actuality they endeavor to define. And while you don't need to stop interpreting, you *can* see the interpretations *as* interpretations and stop mistaking them for truth.

What Is Experience Made Of?

If I were interested in learning what some material object, say a rock, was made of, I could study it and through that investigation discover that the rock is composed of a complex array of cells which are in turn made of unique configurations of molecules composed of billions upon billions of atoms that are themselves composed of all manner of known and unknown subatomic particles, waves, quarks, and so forth.

But just as we seem naturally inclined as human beings to explore the nature and substance of material things, we can also ask the same questions about subjective experience. To be sure, we have a seemingly endless number of ways to describe and categorize the vast array of experiences we encounter. We've even developed complex psychological and neuroscientific models to explain how these different dimensions of subjective experience correlate with and influence one another.

However, the problem with language is that it's a little too facile in so far as it leads us to believe that simply because we have words to describe our experience, we actually know what those experiences *are*.

Sure, we may have many words to describe the things we experience from moment to moment. But what are those words actually made of? What, for example, is fear made of, experientially? What is consciousness, memory, desire, sorrow, or any other experience actually made of? Just as with the example of the rock, if an answer arises, such as, "Well, fear is made of these particular sensations and thoughts," can we look again and ask ourselves the same question: "What are those things I call 'sensations' and 'thoughts' made of?" You can listen to a recording for this chapter at http://www.newharbinger.com/41818.

PRACTICE

For these next few moments, simply feel whatever is here.

It matters not what it is, how it may be appearing, nor how you might be describing it.

Just feel what's present experientially. Now, ask yourself the following: "What is this experience actually made of?"

Don't try to answer it conceptually.

Just feel your way into the question in much the same way that you might feel the texture of wood with your hand or the wind as it blows upon your face. Relax any effort to try to figure out what this flow of experiencing is made of and simply feel the presence of it.

Notice that experience is really too slippery, too unstable, and too transient to ever get a conceptual handle on. And because of this, see that the only thing we can ever actually describe is a memory of what was.

For now, just relax any effort to remember how things were appearing an instant ago or imagine what they might be like in the next instant and instead, simply feel what is here, right now—reality, as it is, unencumbered by whatever we imagine it was or might be. Feel that. Revel in it. Allow yourself to drink deeply from its miraculous waters...

See that there really is no final answer to this question of what experience is made of but only ever this endless free fall into the unfathomable mystery of it all.

The Partiality of All Explanations

Neuroscientists are fond of saying that the sense of being a "self" is created by the brain's activity (Klemm 2011). Now, I'm not saying this view doesn't have some value or utility as a perspective. In fact, it can be quite transformative to realize that this self we've believed to be a substantial thing that can be threatened is actually being spontaneously generated by biochemical and neuronal processes. But the "brain creates self" model is still ultimately a conceptual rendering of an experiential reality that cannot be collapsed into *any* explanatory model, be it scientific, materialistic, spiritual, or metaphysical.

I'm not suggesting that all frameworks are necessarily created equal. But frameworks *are* equivalent in so far as their being necessarily partial or provisional. For example, take the view that the firing of neurons is what creates a sense of being a "me" and that the organism evolved this capacity in order to facilitate its navigation of reality. It sounds, at one level, like a very reasonable and rational explanation. But who is to say the world is even like that? Maybe life is far more chaotic, nonrational, and nonlinear than our little human-centric perspective imagines it to be.

As a causal explanation, we can argue based on the current, limited, and rudimentary understandings of consciousness and human experience being offered by neuroscience that it is the activity of neurons that gives rise to the experience we call being a conscious, separate self. But why stop there? Why not then examine what, if anything, is causing neurons to do what they're doing? In answering the question of how a sense of self comes about, isn't it arbitrary to stop at neurons when we know that what we call a neuron isn't merely what we imagine it to be, composed as it were of all manner of atomic and subatomic particles which are themselves made of who knows what?

Sure, it seems that the self-sense is generated by a brain and its mysterious dance of neurochemical fireworks. But the operative word here is *seems*. Any interpretation of reality is just that, an interpretation. So to say something is this way or that way is to fall prey to the only real illusion, which is to imagine that our interpretations, no matter how scientifically sound, represent actualities. Well, let me qualify that—an interpretation *is* an actuality in so far as being something that is felt, something that's experienced as being present. It's just not the "truth," since we can never get to the final truth about anything, never arrive at the bottom of what anything actually is, and this is the case whether we're talking physics or subjective experience.

The experience of being a self is no less transcendental and indefinable than the realization that the self is a mental or biochemical/electrical construction. All there is, is experience. And experience cannot be collapsed into *any* framework of knowledge, at least not definitively. All we can really say is that things *seem* to be this, that, or the other thing. One hundred years ago, things seemed, according to Newtonian physics and other sciences, to be a certain way. Now, as knowledge and understanding have evolved, they seem to be another way. And in another 100 years, who knows how it will all seem!

It's Not What You Think It Is

Words represent our understandable attempt to characterize the moments of experience. But any description—fear, joy, worry, sorrow, happiness—is inherently limited and imprecise. For while our descriptions are remarkable in their capacity to approximate reality, they can never fully capture it. As natural as it may be for us to utilize language as a way of orienting ourselves and communicating with one another, the problem is that we mistake our linguistic, conceptual approximations of reality *for* reality. We imagine that we know what experiences are, forgetting that we are doing just that—imagining! In other words, we mistake our verbal map for the experiential territory.

PRACTICE

Take any experience and look directly into its nature.

What is fear, what is joy, what is worry, what is awareness, beyond the labels you give them?

Look at your experience, feel the presence of it, and see whether the words you use to describe what's here adequately capture or contain the moment's multidimensional, multilayered, multi-textured nature and character.

Beyond what you think or imagine them to be, what are experiences, actually?

We use language like a kind of shorthand, a useful way to simplify experiences that, in reality, belie easy classification or simplification. And as natural as it may be for us to utilize language and concepts to orient ourselves, create frames of reference, and communicate with one another, the fact of the matter is that our linguistic and conceptual frameworks represent characterizations of a reality that is, by its very nature, impossible to fully characterize.

The myriad frameworks we employ represent interpretations of something that is ultimately uninterpretable, descriptions of things that are essentially indescribable, finite and bounded definitions of experiential realities that are, by nature, infinite and unbounded and therefore incapable of being fully or definitively characterized.

Dialogue: *The Uses and Limitations of Language*

Dave: You encourage people to live more in the "actuality" of their experience rather than relying on their conceptual and linguistic descriptions and interpretations. But aren't you implying that we should stop trying to communicate about our experiences, since it's not actually possible to convey them? What bothers me about this is that it seems we *have* to use language. After all, if we don't communicate with others about our experiences, aren't we just going to end up living inside these little subjective cocoons, harboring our own private, nonverbal realities?

John: To be sure, I'm suggesting that the descriptions and mental interpretations we bring to experience and then share with others through language are limited. Words can't capture reality's complex, multidimensional nature. At the same time, I'm not negating the value and usefulness of trying to describe reality from our limited points of view and then communicating those descriptions to others. Heck, that's what I'm doing with you in this dialogue!

What I *am* saying is that even while we continue to use language to talk about our experience, we can also begin to widen our experiential lens. We can open ourselves to the dimensions of experience that lie beyond words and concepts. We don't need to stop using language. But even as we continue to describe things and share those descriptions with others, we can also begin to appreciate the inherent limitations of our concepts, recognizing that human experience cannot be definitively categorized or captured by *any* of our frameworks.

Just because we have names for things doesn't mean we definitively know what those things are—reality is beyond the reach of our characterizations of it. Life is forever wider, deeper, vaster than our finite concepts and language systems are capable of accommodating. And by recognizing the ways in which reality transcends our notions about it, we can discover something that we often overlook—a profound depth and richness intrinsic to all experience.

Dave: That's very helpful. I find that sharing and speaking with others about my experiences is one of the great pleasures of life. And I don't want to lose that, simply because I've come to discover the limitations of language.

John: As I was saying, part of being language-using creatures is discussing our experiences. And the nature of language means that we use concepts to characterize how reality appears to us. But even as we do this, we can appreciate that experiences are far more open-ended, ambiguous, and ultimately indefinable than language would suggest. And by seeing that we can't pin down reality with any philosophy, meaning-making framework, religion, ideology, or belief system, we discover a profound freedom.

Dave: Freedom? What exactly do you mean?

John: Well, to be stuck in an experience or circumstance, we first have to know what it is. And what I'm saying is that the states we imagine ourselves caught in—fear, anxiety, insecurity, confusion—transcend any and all definitions we might bring to them.

Dave: But what does that have to do with freedom?

John: As we come to taste more directly the multidimensional, non-conceptual nature of every state, we discover that the experiences we thought were solid, fixed things are actually open-ended and indefinite. We find freedom from the experiences that trouble us by seeing they're not actually the bounded, discrete things we imagined them to be. In short, we clarify their nature. We see that we can never get to the bottom of what experiences are. And the more we awaken to the indescribability of everything, the more we begin to taste the inherent freedom and open-endedness of every experience.

Dave: Sure, I think I get what you're saying. But again, aren't you implying that we should somehow stop trying to use language to define and describe things, since that's not actually possible?

John: Actually, there is nothing wrong with using language; it's a rich and important part of human interaction. The problem is not that we use words and concepts to describe things, it's that we imagine those descriptions represent absolute truths rather than mere approximations of reality.

Dave: I see.

John: I don't believe humans will ever stop interacting, loving, playing, and learning together, and language will likely continue to be central in all these endeavors. But if we can recognize the fundamental limitations of language, we can be more open and flexible and less defended about whatever we may believe, and increasingly comfortable with the inherent ambiguity, uncertainty, and indefinability of everything.

As I see it, the point of spiritual or psychological inquiry is to find out what's *true* about experience, to encounter reality *as it is* rather than merely our fantasies, projections, hopes, beliefs, and ideas about it. Every moment, from the subtlest to the most obvious, transcends any effort we might make to characterize it—which doesn't negate the characterizations or descriptions, though it places them in a much vaster context. Language and concepts are facile. "Oh, yeah, I know what that is, it's anxiety or it's joy…"

The conceptual frameworks we use to characterize experience point to *something* that is concretely present. The question is, what exactly *is* that?

Reality, the Greatest Drug of All

Not too long ago, a client said to me during a Skype session, "It sounds from the way you are describing the nature of experience that you're on ayahuasca or something." I had to laugh, letting her know that the last drug I ingested was probably some 35 years ago! I said to her that we are, in a very real sense, already "tripping" on the greatest drug of all, experience itself. To be sure, we may imagine otherwise, that this reality we find ourselves experiencing is anything but an inspiring trip; it may even seem quite dull or boring at times (or much of the time). It may appear as if nothing is going on that we would call extraordinary or awe-inspiring. But could it be that we're not looking carefully enough? Maybe we have just grown accustomed to defining experiences in particular ways, blind, as it were, to the inconceivable miracle that is unfolding as every momentary experience. Is there a way to see this more clearly, to awaken more fully to the astounding, remarkable nature of everything?

Try out the practice below or listen to a recording for this chapter at http://www.newharbinger.com/41818.

PRACTICE

For these next few minutes, I invite you to peer around the edges of your descriptions of things, just beyond the horizon of your seeming certainty and knowledge of what things are. Just let yourself explore whatever is presenting itself experientially—the sounds of traffic, the splashes of flickering color everywhere, the sometimes gentle, sometimes chaotic flow of thoughts and feelings rushing by. It matters not what is actually here; just let yourself trip on it, marveling at the way everything moves, the way experience unfolds, the way each perceptual phenomenon dances and sparkles and shines—the color, the light, the shape, the texture, the flavor, the energy that appears spontaneously as each flash instant of life. Let yourself trip on the way that experience never holds still. Notice how the moment is instantaneously present, suddenly here with no clear beginning or end.

Allow yourself to be taken in, captivated, and entranced by even the most seemingly unimportant or meaningless things showing up in the field of experience—a crack in the sidewalk, a glint of light on your armchair, the dance of shadow and light playing on the wall, the grains of wood on the kitchen table, a tiny, insignificant blade of grass or dead leaf that has fallen to the ground. Let yourself trip on all of it, falling into the endlessly amazing nature of everything that's being experienced—every thought, every sound, every sight, every feeling, every sensation, all of it a complete marvel, every moment a trip into bottomless infinity.

Through this kind of investigation, you can begin to taste the way in which experience—without the aid of any mind-altering substances—is always and already a total trip, an infinitely diverse, kaleidoscopic array and mix of color, light, texture, nuance, energy, and consciousness…an indescribable, richly textured, wildly unpredictable, dynamic flashing forth of phenomena…a ceaseless, ungraspable, unnameable flow of sparkling sensations, feelings, thoughts, perceptions, memories…a shining, flickering, shape-shifting, morphing dance…a presence that is always here, always now, yet never the same…a singular, seamless, undivided reality that is, at the same time, unimaginably colorful and diverse. Experience, as it is: the greatest drug of all!

The Confirmation Bias

One of the most important discoveries made in the field of psychology over the past few decades is the *confirmation bias*. This perceptual bias refers to our tendency to search out information that confirms our preconceived notions about the world and ignore or overlook those bits of data that don't fit our prior assumptions. The confirmation bias reflects our deep-seated habit and inclination to defend whatever we believe to be true regardless of any disconfirming evidence we might be presented with.

The reality is that in any given moment, we don't really experience life as it is; we experience our beliefs, interpretations, and descriptions of life. We are, in a very real sense, hypnotized by our beliefs and ideologies about everything, caught up in the web of our own descriptions, living inside a virtual world made of concepts, not reality. We believe our descriptions, imagining they represent reality when, in fact, they are necessarily crude approximations of this unfathomably rich, multidimensional complexity we call life.

It's all very innocent and natural, this impulse to create explanations and develop various models of reality. It's understandable that we humans would desire to create some sense of order, certainty, and predictability in the face of the sea of uncertainty and unpredictability we find ourselves swimming in. The problem, however (and human history illustrates this quite clearly and painfully), is that we all too often become personally and emotionally invested, imagining our conceptual maps and interpretive renderings to be true representations of reality. And it is right there where we can see the power of the confirmation bias at work, making it that much harder for us to see beyond our cherished notions, frameworks, and explanatory models, hesitant to truly open ourselves up and consider the possibility that things may be far richer and far more nuanced and multi-dimensional than we've imagined them to be.

It's fairly easy to see the ways in which the confirmation bias has served to perpetuate such things as racial and gender stereotyping and prejudice. Its powerful role in human conflict is also quite clear. Whether religious, political, or ideological in nature, our resistance to having our points of view challenged seems to know no bounds. But not only do we cling to and defend our viewpoints regarding the world, politics, religion, and so forth—we also subscribe to all manner of beliefs and ideas about our own subjective experience, taking for granted that the words we use to describe what appears are somehow "true" characterizations of whatever may be occurring.

Let's take the term "tired." Tired is really an abstraction, a conceptual rendering of what is essentially a momentary, fleeting set of perceptions and sensations. The use of any word, including "tired," represents an understandable yet ultimately futile attempt to capture in language the myriad textures and patterns that constitute human experience. To be sure, the use of language can function at one level to help distinguish one type of patterning of life energy ("tired") from another (such as "exhilarated"). But if we investigate any experience, in this example feeling tired, we'll find that "tired" isn't exactly what we imagine it to be. Beyond the label we give it, beyond the verbal descriptor, what exactly is this flow of experience we describe as "tired"? Can we really say? When we inquire into it experientially, when we dive directly into the raw energy of this thing called "being tired" rather than reflexively referring to the conceptual label to tell us what the experience is, we are left with something far less definite, something in fact quite elusive, a set of experiential phenomena that, while totally present and undeniable, is at the same time impossible to grasp hold of or pin down definitively. To be sure, things appear, and we have descriptive labels that we use to refer to them. But the reality is that each momentary perception utterly transcends any effort to define or characterize it.

Another way to understand this is that every moment is both conceptual and nonconceptual in nature. Everything that is experienced has its descriptive label, such as "tired," "fearful," "happy," or "anxious," on the one hand and yet at the same time, each of these phenomena is, in fact, utterly beyond our capacity to describe it fully. Put another way, we could say that every experiential phenomenon has two aspects—its sheer existence or presence and its description. At a descriptive level, such things as fear, tiredness, and joy certainly exist. However, these things are, at the same time, unknowable, beyond any possibility of being fully captured descriptively. In other words, we can never quite get to the bottom of what things are.

Now this may all sound terribly abstract and lacking in any sort of practical relevance to our lives. But consider this—the very states such as fear, sorrow, insecurity, anxiety, discomfort, and uncertainty that have plagued and tormented human beings for millennia are not, in fact, merely what they appear to be. We've imagined that these momentary flashes of experiencing labeled as fear or anxiety require some remedy, fix, or cure. But what fuels this persistent view is our belief in the substantive nature of such states, the idea that they are actually "things" that can harm us. And this belief is a direct product of the ways in which such experiential patterns are characterized, conceptually and linguistically, including the myriad stories we layer on top of such phenomena, most notably the idea that such states are problematic in the first place!

Because we have words and definitions for things and experiences, we imagine that we know definitively what these actually are:

"Oh yes, I know what tired is. It's, well…a feeling."

"Okay, but what is a feeling?"

"Well, it's a set of distinct sensations in the body."

"All right then, but what is a sensation?"

"Well…hmm…I'm not exactly sure. It's kind of hard to define or describe, actually…"

"Exactly!"

At one level, reality is precisely what we say it is. Tired is tired. Fear is fear. Happiness is happiness, and so on. At the same time, our experiences are forever transcending any effort we might make to explain, define, or otherwise characterize them. And so we find ourselves smack dab in the middle of this beautiful, awe-inspiring paradox—we know what things are on the one hand (their descriptive labels), and yet we also don't know what they are, for everything is inherently uncertain and indeterminate. All that exists is pure, wide-open, ungraspable mystery, through and through.

Understandably, we cling to our explanatory models and labels, falling prey to the confirmation bias, because they give us some sense of safety, security, and certainty. It can no doubt be a somewhat scary, even terrifying proposition to consider that we could allow our points of view to be held lightly as frames of reference, rather than absolute truths existing in their own right.

PRACTICE

For a moment, consider that despite all our seeming knowledge, all the mental interpretations we habitually bring to the moments of our lives, the ideas, beliefs, opinions, speculations, philosophies, conceptual maps and models, we don't actually know what experience is, at least not definitively (which is a euphemism for not at all)!

Experience is simply too complex to be understood by the thoughts that are generated about it; there is just too much detail, too much information, too much complexity, too much nuance, too much subtlety to accurately render this moment via the mechanism of thought.

Let yourself feel the truth of this unknowability, the impossibility of being able to say precisely what this moment of experience actually is.

Let yourself feel the ways in which your thoughts about what is occurring fail to capture the inconceivable depth that is actually present.

For a brief moment, just let all your knowledge, all the definitions, all the mental maps and interpretations fall away. The seemingly firm, predictable ground of knowing that you once imagined could be counted on—just let that give way, for it can't really hold you or this moment anyway.

The concepts, definitions, and descriptions we bring to this are partial at best. Of course we long to know what this is, to stand upon the firm ground of our thoughts about reality. And yet the truth is that we're in an exhilarating free fall of indeterminacy and multidimensionality, never quite landing anywhere firm.

And yet right there is our greatest liberation, the freedom from any and all fixed frameworks. Our labels, definitions, and conceptualizations may have brought us an imagined security. But the true security, the true ground, is really no ground at all. This is a *groundless ground*, every miraculous instant known yet unfathomable, experienced yet ungraspable.

Distinguishing Thought from Experience

As I've been saying, we live, in a sense, in two worlds, the world of direct experience and the world of our thoughts and ideas *about* that experience. And our tendency is to confuse the two, lumping them together and imagining that experience is what we think it is. This mistaking our conceptual rendering of reality *for* reality turns out to be the source of much of our confusion.

To further highlight the difference between these two realms—experience and the interpretations we bring to it—here is a meditation. You can also download a recording of it at http://www.newharbinger.com/41818.

PRACTICE

For the next few moments, simply feel the experience conventionally labeled as "breathing."

Just sense all that is present, the incredibly rich array of textures that constitute what we call the breath.

Now go ahead and let yourself formulate whatever concepts the mind is inclined to generate about the experience of breathing—what it is, how it works, its various qualities, for example its depth or shallowness. Just notice whatever characterizations of the breath may be present, including the name we give it.

Next, simply notice both the direct experience of this thing called breathing and any thoughts you might be having about it. And now, notice the way in which these two dimensions—the direct experience and your interpretation of what it is—function independently of one another.

For example, the set of experiential textures and qualities that make up what you call the breath are what they are, irrespective of how you might describe them. Similarly, the direct, raw, unfiltered experience of these textural qualities in no way interferes with the mental interpretations you bring to them.

See that the experience called breathing does not actually come with any label attached to it.

No definition or description is intrinsic to the experience. The experience and the thoughts about it exist side by side, with neither intruding upon the other.

Now let yourself feel the complex, intricate set of phenomena we call "the body." Notice the swirling array of sensations and energies that are present.

And now bring awareness to the ideas you may be having about this dynamic display. See that the label itself ("body") is merely an idea, a way of conceptually designating whatever is being experienced.

Again, notice these two realms—the direct experience and the thoughts you have about it—and see the way in which they do not interfere with one another but exist, in a sense, in their own separate domains.

The intricate, complex dance of energies we conventionally label as "body" are what they are, irrespective of whatever we might think about them.

Lastly, if you were to characterize what is happening right now, you might say something along the lines of, "Well, I'm sitting here, reading or listening to these words and practicing this guided meditation."

See that description as a description, an effort to make conceptual sense of what's happening.

And now feel what is *actually* present in the field of experience, this explosion of light, color, sound, and energy, this wildly unpredictable, uncontrollable dance of flickering sensations, memories, thoughts, feelings, and images.

See the narrative about what you imagine is happening here. And now feel the actuality that description pretends to capture, appreciating the ways in which the one is not the other.

Categories

Essentially, categories don't exist, at least not as actualities; they are conceptual abstractions. For example, take the category "flowers." Flowers represent a class of things which share certain characteristics. However, in order to place the obviously unique objects we call a rose, a marigold, and a tulip in the same conceptual category, we must overlook those distinctive features such as shape, color, and texture we consider to be nonessential elements of the category. This perceptual censorship enables us to create the myriad abstract, conceptual categories we are all quite familiar with.

Let's look at another category of phenomena, a rose. If you were to take any two objects conventionally labeled as "roses," they'd undoubtedly share certain features that allow us to group them together conceptually. However, if we look carefully, it can be seen that even if the roses are very similar in terms of size, shape, color, petal formation, and so on, no rose is ever precisely the same as another.

And so, that beautiful red object you see growing in your garden—even if you might have a conventional word to describe it, a closer look reveals that you can't say precisely what it is owing to its distinctive nature; it's literally in a class by itself. Even if there exist other objects that appear to resemble it, there is nothing quite like *this* one. Given that this thing we call a "rose" is uniquely itself, to place it in some general category of things is to oversimplify the unthinkable complexity that it actually exhibits. When we look at what we conventionally call a rose, the reality is that we're not really looking at a rose; we are looking at something we've never actually seen before. For no matter how closely it may appear to resemble other things, that which we're viewing is an utterly unique configuration of shape, color, and texture. And so only by censoring or overlooking its uniquely distinctive features are we able to categorize anything.

PRACTICE

As you sit here, try to characterize, in a word or two, your predominant state of mind at this moment. Whatever your word is (calmness, agitation, elation, confusion, fatigue, joy), just note it silently to yourself.

Now, let's say your word is "fatigue." Like every other description, fatigue represents our attempt to characterize what is ultimately an inconceivably complex pattern of perceptual phenomena. An experience appears, which we then recognize in some way as having arisen before: "Oh, I know what *that* is, it's fatigue (or whatever your word was)." But actually, while the pattern we're experiencing is certainly reminiscent of something we've encountered before, it is not the same as any previous perceptual moment. At least not exactly...

With that notion in mind, just feel your present experience, however you may be labeling it.

Sure, it may seem as if you can place it in some category as I suggested. But can you sense how complex and multidimensional, how ultimately uncharacterizable and utterly unique this experience actually is?

Can you feel how, even if it has certain familiar features and characteristics that remind you of other moments like it, the experience is unlike anything you've ever felt or encountered before?

The reality is that each experience is unique. It belongs to *no* category, owing to its completely original nature.

So what does this all mean? Well, it points to the fact that because no two moments are exactly alike, there is no actual reference point to know what anything or any experience is. This flash instant that's appearing has, quite literally, never come into existence before, at least not exactly like this. Every moment is a complete original! And so experiences cannot be known, cannot be named, cannot be conceptualized or categorized without overlooking so much of the depth and detail that makes each instant the utterly unique expression of life that it is.

Yes, we can name and categorize things in order to make sense of ourselves and the world and communicate with each other. But even as we continue to do this, which we likely will until our final breath, we can appreciate that experience cannot fit neatly into any of our categories or concepts. It's simply too big, too complex, too multifaceted for that.

And just as objects (such as roses) and experiences (such as fatigue) are too vast and multidimensional to be held by our categories and names, so too are we. We are not what we were a year, a month, or even a second ago; we are, like every other phenomenon, ever-changing from moment to moment, even if in barely perceptible ways. And because of this, defining or categorizing ourselves is not actually possible without overlooking our inherently dynamic nature.

Who we are is literally not who we were even a nanosecond ago. Any definitions of who and what we are could only ever be based on memory, on some image or idea of ourselves. But that is simply not what we are *now*. Because reality is inherently unstable and impermanent, we are, quite literally, beyond definition, beyond any possibility of being categorized according to any set of seemingly stable qualities or characteristics. What we are is *this* actuality, *this* reality arising right now in a way it has never before arisen.

Dialogue: *Discovering the Common Denominator*

Ingrid: I was listening to an interview in which you were describing the existence of "another order of well-being." Can you explain what you mean by that term?

John: Sure. Ordinarily, we equate a sense of well-being with the presence of certain body-mind states such as happiness and pleasure and the absence of others such as fear, sadness, and anxiety. Given human beings' seemingly universal desire to experience well-being, it's not surprising that we would try to arrange our lives in such a way as to maximize those states and circumstances we associate with well-being while avoiding or minimizing those we deem to be lacking in it.

Ingrid: Yes, that makes logical sense and certainly describes my own experience trying to realize greater well-being in my life.

John: Yes, this approach to well-being certainly has a strong intuitive appeal. However, it also has a number of significant downsides. Foremost among these is the fact that despite our best efforts, we're frequently unable to effectively control our experiences and circumstances. As a result, we end up encountering all manner of things that lead us to feel we're somehow lacking in well-being, experiencing either too many moments that are not to our liking or not enough of the ones that we like.

Ingrid: Are you saying it's wrong to seek circumstances that bring us pleasure and avoid those we'd rather not experience?

John: Not at all. That search is fine and natural, as far as it goes.

Ingrid: As far as it goes?

John: There's certainly nothing wrong with taking whatever steps we can to secure more of the states we enjoy and less of those that we'd rather not experience. But it's arguably a fool's errand to imagine we could realize any degree of consistent, stable, or predictable happiness through such a strategy.

Ingrid: Why do you say that?

John: Because it's not really possible to find anything truly stable and lasting in experiences and circumstances that are by nature unstable and impermanent.

Ingrid: I see. But does that mean we're doomed to this hamster wheel existence, chasing after experiences and circumstances that feel good, trying our best to avoid those that don't, and failing to consistently achieve either?

John: Well, as I like to say, there are really two ways to approach this. The most familiar is what we've been discussing, doing what we can to maximize pleasurable and fulfilling experiences while avoiding those we find lacking in pleasure and fulfillment. As I said, we're free to continue to engage with life this way. But there's another way and that is discovering what doesn't come and go but is continuous.

Ingrid: I'm confused. You frequently say that experiences are constantly changing, that it's not really possible to hold on to thoughts, feelings, sensations, and circumstances owing to their dynamic, impermanent nature. But if experiences are always changing, what do you mean when you say we can discover a well-being that is unchanging or continuous?

John: You're absolutely right that a well-being described as continuous can't be found in things which are, by nature, discontinuous. In that realm, we imagine well-being depends upon what's being experienced and the way in which that is being defined. But there's another place we can go, a realm or dimension of well-being and fulfillment that is not dependent upon what's happening.

Ingrid: Not dependent upon what's happening?

John: As we've been exploring, experiences do not last and as a result, it's simply not possible to find any sort of lasting happiness in them. However, despite their inherently unstable, impermanent nature, experiences, from the most pleasurable and enjoyable to the most difficult and painful, do share a common denominator. And it is there where we can go to find this other order or dimension of well-being I'm speaking about.

Ingrid: But you also talk about the way in which every experience is utterly unique. So how can experiences have a common denominator?

John: Good question! It's true that every moment that appears is utterly distinct from anything else that has come before it. So yes, each experience, each appearance of life is indeed like no other. But every moment shares one thing in common, and that is its very existence.

Ingrid: Okay. But what does that have to do with well-being?

John: We could say that every experience has two fundamental dimensions. There is the description of whatever appears, and then there is the sheer presence or existence of it. The experiences we define as joyful and clear are, without question, distinct from those we describe as sad or confused. And it's fine and understandable to prefer some states over others and then seek to have more of the ones we prefer. But what I'm suggesting is that there's another dimension of well-being that resides in the sheer presence and existence of things rather than in their descriptions.

Ingrid: I don't get it…how can the presence of something painful and difficult be a source of well-being?

John: The answer is that we only discover this other dimension of well-being by leaving behind the world of descriptions, if even for a brief moment.

Ingrid: You mean we stop describing things?

John: No, I'm not suggesting we should or even can cease labeling and defining things. That's a natural function of human consciousness, it would appear! But this other domain of well-being I'm talking about lies entirely beyond the realm of human description. Unlike the well-being that's tied to the world of descriptions and labels, this is a well-being that has no opposite.

Ingrid: No opposite?

John: The states we describe as "happy" and "fulfilled" are essentially defined in terms of their opposites, that is *not happy* and *not fulfilled*. The realm of the described is, we could say, the realm of opposed frameworks. It's the realm of distinctions, the domain of *this* versus *that*, of happiness versus unhappiness, clarity versus confusion, joy versus sorrow, and so on. But as I said, all states and circumstances, while absolutely distinct at the level of their description, are at the same time completely equal in terms of their existence. This is the common denominator I'm pointing to. Regardless of the myriad ways we might characterize the moments that visit us, they share one common feature and that is the fact of their presence, the fact that they *are*. And that turns out to be a powerful, astounding fact.

Ingrid: Powerful? How so?

John: Unlike the realm of the described which is constantly coming and going, not to mention wildly unpredictable, the dimension of presence *doesn't* come and go. Experiences and circumstances are constantly changing; sometimes we like them, sometimes we don't. But they are *always* present. The presence of things never changes; we can count on that fact. Presence is, we could say, the one thing that *is* reliable, the one thing that is constant. Something is always present, always here, even if that which is present and here is forever changing!

Ingrid: But how do we access this other realm, the realm of the undescribed?

John: In the realm of the described, we have to employ all manner of strategies in order to realize moments we equate with well-being while simultaneously doing whatever we can to keep at bay those we consider to be lacking in well-being. But in the realm of sheer presence, there exists no opposite. There is only ever the presence of what is, and while its particular flavor is forever changing, presence remains as it is: present...

For this reason, no effort is required to change either our experiences or circumstances for presence to be. Presence is, no matter the form it may be taking. And so rather than teaching methods to get ourselves more connected to presence, I'm simply pointing to the fact that it's impossible to ever leave it!

Ingrid: That's powerful, to know that there is something that is always here, always present.

John: Yes, it is! Now many people get confused and imagine that feeling a sense of presence is a particular experience they can either have or not have. This is a subtle but important point I want to emphasize.

We can certainly recognize that the moments of life are present, regardless of how we might describe them; we can see that presence is not dependent upon whatever experiential content may be showing up. We can realize that sorrow is no less present than joy or that frustration is no less present than satisfaction. And as an experience, this is a powerful and liberating thing to realize, to discover that existence continues to exist, that presence remains present no matter how it may appear or be defined.

In a moment of insight, we can feel the presence of presence and recognize that presence can never be absent for it is the fundamental nature of everything that appears, including experiences we might label as lacking in presence! However, like every other experience that may arise, the moments of recognizing that presence can never actually disappear will themselves disappear. It's quite paradoxical!

Ingrid: But you just said that presence is continuous, that it never comes and goes. So if that's true, how can it ever disappear?

John: As I said, this is a very subtle point. Yes, presence is continuous for it is the nature of every experiential moment to be present, by definition. But the experiential recognition that this is the case, that presence is here and can never depart, can and will fade, just as all experiences inevitably do. And when that occurs, when we find ourselves feeling as if presence has somehow vanished, that we've lost touch with it, we will naturally seek out ways to regain that experience of presence we imagine has been lost.

Ingrid: I see. But the experience we describe as *lacking in presence* is still present, right?

John: Exactly! Even the feeling that we have somehow lost contact with presence is fully, one hundred percent present! This is what begins to dawn, that even though described experiences are forever coming and going—for that is their nature, to never last—presence remains, existence remains, appearing in all the infinite guises that it does.

              What's crucial to realize in all of this is that presence (call it life or existence if you prefer) is not dependent upon the myriad ways it can appear. That's what makes it so powerful! Simply put, presence does not depend upon whatever happens to be present, for it is the nature of *all* things to be present.

Ingrid: That's amazing! Are there any other ways this can be pointed to?

John: Yes. I often use the word "being." Regardless of how something is described, it *is*. Everything exists, everything is, even if *this that is*, is forever on the move. We could call this the *beingness* or *isness* of everything.

              Another word that could be used is "now." Now continues to be now, irrespective of how it may be showing up. Now is invulnerable; it's impossible to destroy it, even as it is continuously dying and being reborn as the next instant, the next *now*...

              Another word I sometimes use is "experiencing." As we've been discussing, experiences are forever coming and going. But the fact of experiencing itself is continuous. It never stops.

Experiences are constantly appearing and then disappearing, but the light of experiencing itself never turns off.

We can also use the word "knowing." Whatever is being known—that's the realm of the described; sometimes we know what we could call happiness and sometimes we know sadness. But the *knowing* is constant; knowing is the ever-present, common denominator underlying whatever is being known. The content of what's known is forever changing. But the knowing itself remains, fundamentally untouched and unchanged by whatever is being known.

Ingrid: So then, all of these different words are really just synonyms for this common denominator you're speaking of?

John: Yes. And as we become increasingly familiar with this common element of every experience, another realm of well-being and fulfillment is revealed, one that is realized to be independent of whatever is occurring. We come to see that while finding any sort of stable well-being in that which is inherently unstable (the coming and going of experience) is a dicey proposition, stability *can* be found in that which doesn't come and go, *the fact of experiencing itself.*

So, just let yourself play with all of this, allowing yourself periodic moments during the day to gently shift attention from the content of whatever is being experienced to the simple fact of its presence, the fact that it is. Revel in this. Feel how liberating it is to know and touch this presence of experiencing that remains, no matter how it may be appearing.

Interpretive Frameworks

A caption placed beneath a picture tells us something about what we're seeing. But no matter how clever it might be, captions can never hope to convey the infinite depth and detail of information contained in any visual image. Thoughts, whether about people, places, or things, are very much like captions. For what I imagine or conceive about you, however accurate that may be, is not the same as what you *actually* are; what I think or say a given experience is ("that's happiness, that's fear, that's a tree, that's loneliness...") is never the same as its incomprehensibly rich and complex actuality.

You can listen to a recording of the following practice at http://www.newharbinger.com/41818.

PRACTICE

As you sit here, notice that without any real effort on your part, interpretations and descriptions of experience are being generated spontaneously.

Just let yourself feel whatever is being felt, sense whatever is being sensed, notice whatever is being noticed and as you do so, appreciate that the mind is trying to wrap its head around what's here, trying to characterize it, trying to make sense of and determine what it is by labeling and defining it.

But as you appreciate this natural function of consciousness to interpret experience, see if you can also notice how impossible it is to fully capture experience in any of the definitions or descriptions being generated about it.

Feel what is present, notice the effort to make sense of and interpret it and then see how inadequate those interpretations are, how impossible it is to really say what this is that's occurring, the profound mystery that is every momentary perception.

Experience Deviates from Our Interpretations

There are many things that we believe, that we take for granted as being real, whether about the world or ourselves. Call it conventional reality, if you like. We imagine that things have a kind of stable, static nature, that there is a permanence, a continuity, a coherence to things, that the people, places, and things we experience are more or less what they were a moment ago. We don't, for example, question whether time is real, believing whole-heartedly that the categories of past, present, and future actually exist as real, discernible, irrefutable things.

And just as we have no doubt that time exists, so do we believe in this thing called space, never really questioning the presumption that we are "here" while the world which is not us exists over "there." But let's take a moment and investigate these largely unquestioned assumptions, exploring the ways in which the world of immediate, direct experience actually deviates from so many of our conventionally held notions. You can find a recording of the following practice at http://www.newharbinger.com/41818.

PRACTICE

Look in your immediate experience... Can you actually find an "inside?" Can you tell exactly where "here" is as opposed to that which we conventionally label as "there?"

If so, where is the dividing line? Where does this supposed inside (here) end and the purported outside (over there) begin?

To be sure, we believe these distinctions to be true and actual. But *are* they?

Look at experience itself: Can any lines or seams actually be found? Are the apparent divisions actually there or might these seeming lines between inside and outside be merely imagined?

Now let's look at this thing we call time. Look in experience... Can you identify a clear beginning to any experience that appears? Can you locate an actual past?

Where does that supposed "before" exist other than in this mysterious thing we call memory? Where does what we call the past end and the "present moment" begin? And where does what we call "now" cease to exist and start to become the next thing (the future)?

We imagine that experiences have continuity, that they endure over time. But look and see if anything actually lasts.

Notice that experiences never actually repeat themselves, that each flash instant is utterly distinct from the next. Notice that experiences don't actually have duration, that every thought, feeling, and sensation vanishes no sooner than it appears. Appreciate how dynamic experience is, how whatever is appearing is forever changing, never holding still for even a second.

The Vast and Indescribable Nature of Experience

Experience does not come with a label or name tag pinned to its lapel, announcing what it is. The dance of light and color in the evening sky does not say, "I'm a sunset." The clear, sparkling liquid racing down the mountainside doesn't announce to us, "I'm a river." No, it is *we* who supply the labels. Experience arrives *as it is*, presenting as various qualities, characteristics, attributes, and textures. And those very qualities that make up what we call experience also come with no narrative attached. They arrive naked and unadorned by any ideas we might entertain about them.

Now, most of us have experienced the way in which certain moments such as listening to music, making love, or seeing some awesome display of nature are beyond the reach of words. We recognize that such moments are simply too vast, too rich, and too multifaceted to be captured by any of our descriptive frameworks. But as it turns out, this is the case with *all* experience. Let's explore...

PRACTICE

As you sit here, pick any aspect of experience—the feeling of the breath moving in and out of the body, the complex array of sounds you hear, the intricate play of light all around you—whatever is presenting itself most noticeably, just feel how vast and indescribable it actually is.

Notice the ways in which your ideas about whatever is being experienced, the labels you apply to each moment, are so limited, so much less rich and detailed than the experiences themselves.

For example, the thing sitting here that we call "the body"—notice how that concept could never hope to contain the vast kaleidoscope of sensations cascading through consciousness each instant.

Feel the unthinkably complex dance of energies that constitute each moment of experience and appreciate the ways in which no words, no concepts, no descriptions can encompass the actuality of whatever is here.

Dialogue: *Are You Saying That Suffering Isn't Real?*

Tim: When I hear you speak about experience, it sometimes sounds like you're denying the reality of human suffering. You seem to be implying that the pain we experience in ourselves and see happening in the larger world isn't actually real but is merely imagined, defined into existence through the medium of language and conceptualization. But what about things like torture, abuse, and severe psychological trauma? Are you saying those don't really exist, that their negative effects and implications are merely the result of interpretation? Isn't this dismissive of people's actual suffering?

John: In all that I write and speak about, I am certainly not suggesting that whatever is presenting itself experientially or circumstantially isn't at times exceedingly difficult to navigate.

Just to give a personal example, several months ago, totally out of the blue, I developed severe pain in my wrist. While I'm still not entirely clear what caused this flare-up, it was probably the most severe pain I've ever experienced in this life. It literally brought me to my knees in tears, several times over the course of the weeks it was occurring. Nothing that I did seemed to reduce the pain, including taking very powerful steroids. Needless to say, if someone were to ask me at the time what that experience was like, I would have described it as a very challenging and painful situation. It certainly wasn't anything I would have wished on another, nor was it something I hoped to experience in the future!

And so in part because that experience was as intense and unrelenting as it was, despite my best efforts to resolve it, I decided to spend some time exploring what it was.

Tim: What do you mean, *what it was*? You just said it was intensely painful and difficult to deal with. So, isn't *painful* and *difficult* exactly what that experience was?

John: Well, yes and no. I'm not denying the reality of the pain that was being felt. That word certainly conveys, at least at one level, what was being experienced. However, what I was investigating during that time, and invite others to explore in my work, is what the "raw material" of experience is.

Tim: The raw material?

John: Yes. When a circumstance conventionally labeled as painful or difficult arises, what exactly are those labels referring to? Some complex array of phenomena is undoubtedly present, which we then label as pain or discomfort. But while these descriptors indicate *something* about what is happening, the words don't tell us much about the details that make up such descriptions. And so the question I asked myself and am asking you now is, what is pain *actually* composed of, experientially? What is the raw material that constitutes pain, whether physical or emotional?

Tim: Well, it's hard to describe. To be honest, I'm not really sure what pain is exactly. I just know it hurts!

John: Fair enough. But when you say, "it hurts," what is the *it* in that phrase referring to?

Tim: I guess I would say *it* refers to a set of feelings or sensations that I find uncomfortable.

John: Okay. But let's probe a little further. What is it that makes that sensorial experience uncomfortable? Put another way, what is the word *discomfort* pointing to in direct experience? To be sure, pain and discomfort are interpretations of something that is happening. The question is, what exactly is it that's occurring that we subsequently label as "painful?"

Tim: I'm not really sure.

John: I can very much appreciate that answer as I'm not really sure myself! When I pose that question, I'm inviting you to examine what you might call the non-narrative dimensions of experience. We're all very familiar with the narrative dimensions, those descriptive labels we use to tell ourselves and others about what is happening.

But what do the descriptions we use refer *to*? The answer to this question reveals the non-narrative, nonconceptual dimensions of experience, those aspects of reality that lie beyond the reach of words, concepts, and labels. For example, if you look at the set of phenomena I was experiencing with my wrist, there was on the one hand the narration about what was happening: "I can't believe how uncomfortable this is; this pain is excruciating; I'm not sure I can deal with it much longer; why is this happening to me; when is it going to resolve itself," and so on.

But even as there was this ongoing commentary about what was happening, as I explored the more nonverbal, textural dimensions of the experience, I saw that what was being called *pain* was not merely what I thought it was. What I was describing no doubt had its own unique signature, we could say, a certain qualitative feel and texture that was distinct from what I might have called pleasure or comfort. At the same time, I could see that this thing I was calling pain really wasn't a fixed, bounded thing at all but a dynamic, ever-morphing, wavelike movement of energy and information, a universe of inconceivable depth for which there were no words.

Tim: Okay, that sounds intriguing. But did it still hurt? I mean, you may have opened up to another dimension of the pain. But it continued to be experienced as painful, didn't it?

John: Well, it's paradoxical. In many respects, there was still what I would characterize as pain being experienced. And yet, I recognized that what I was calling pain was also far subtler, more nuanced and open-ended than that label typically implies. Yes, I would say my wrist still hurt. At the same time, venturing into those sensations I was describing as painful was like traveling down a deep, dark, bottomless well of indescribability.

Ironically, the more carefully I explored the pain, the less clear I became about what precisely it was. Something was obviously there. But what exactly that was, I cannot really say for it's not really possible to pinpoint, in words or concepts, where or what the wavelike "particles" that constitute the pain experience are composed of. In the end, what we call pain is, like every other experiential phenomenon, an unfathomable, ungraspable mystery, through and through.

Tim: So discovering this other non-narrative, nonconceptual dimension of pain may not have made the pain go away. But it altered your overall experience of it in some way?

John: Yes, very much so. Here's one way to understand the pragmatic value of this inquiry I'm describing. How we see and experience a given phenomenon depends on the particular interpretive frameworks we bring to it. And any experience we encounter in life can be seen from a multitude of perspectives. What I'm suggesting is that along with the myriad ways we can view or make sense conceptually of experiences, we can also become acquainted with what might be termed the *view of inconceivability*.

Tim: The view of inconceivability? I don't understand.

John: Well, one common view of pain is that it's an awful thing that we wish would just go away. Another interpretation might be that the pain is providing us with important information about aspects of our bodies or minds that may be out of balance.

        However, there is another view we can bring to bear upon the difficult to navigate experiences of life, one that lies completely outside the realm of *any* interpretive framework. As I've been saying, this view can be realized by inquiring into the non-narrative dimensions of experience and discovering a kind of perspective-less perspective, one that is radically open-ended and ultimately indefinable.

        Through this inquiry, we come to see that pain is, at least from one vantage, utterly inconceivable. For despite the many ways we humans make sense of and characterize the difficulties encountered in life, we can never quite get to the bottom of what any of those experiences, including pain, are. From one perspective, we know and can describe what physical or emotional pain is. But from another vantage, we can't really say *what* it is…

Tim: And why again is discovering this "perspective-less perspective" so valuable in terms of helping us navigate difficult experiences or circumstances?

John: Well, discovering the ways in which phenomena such as pain transcend our conceptualizations of them frees us up to encounter them much more open-endedly, more flexibly and less rigidly. The feeling of being stuck, trapped, or imprisoned by difficult circumstances or experiences starts to loosen up as we discover the ways in which those challenging states, conventionally thought of as "things" that we can actually *be* stuck in or victimized by, are not actually "things" at all owing to their ever-changing, dynamic, indefinable nature.

Tim: So, while you're not denying the existence of pain, you *are* suggesting that pain is much more than what we conceive it to be and through opening ourselves to its more transcendental, indefinable dimensions, difficult or painful experiences become easier to navigate. Do I have that right?

John: Yes, that's precisely what I am saying. By seeing that the pain could not be captured by any of my conceptual frameworks, I touched that dimension of the pain experience that was free of being a problem.

Tim: No longer a problem? I'm confused. It still sounds like you're denying its reality somehow.

John: Again, it's paradoxical. From one perspective, yes, the pain in my wrist was most certainly still a problem, one that I continued to seek out solutions for. However, from another vantage, I couldn't actually define what that pain was. The experience was quite literally beyond comprehension, an inconceivable mystery, a lightning storm of intermittent flashes of…well, I can't really say what. I guess I'd say that pain is a kind of complex energy presence. But like all descriptors, those words utterly fail to capture the subtle nature and essence of it.

The point is that when pain or any other challenging experience is recognized to be beyond all possible conceptualizations, it ceases to be a problem, even if paradoxically we might continue to take steps to resolve it as I did with my still hurting wrist.

Tim: That makes sense. Thanks…

John: Let me add one more thing here. As we open up and begin exploring the non-narrative dimensions of experience, we can also begin to appreciate that in any given moment in which we're encountering some difficult thing, countless other phenomena are occurring within the field of experience that have absolutely zero connection to the event we're labeling as painful or difficult.

Tim: What do you mean?

John: Well, imagine yourself experiencing some painful situation. Let's say that a very significant relationship, one you've invested a lot of yourself in, suddenly ends. In the immediate wake of this, you find yourself thrust into emotional turmoil, feeling the very raw loss of this important relationship, and the reality of no longer having this person in your life as an intimate friend and partner.

Now, picture the flood of these confusing and painful thoughts and feelings like a whirlpool but as you do so, see this swirling pool of difficult energy as one infinitesimally small, really microscopic part of a vast and boundless sea. This is the reality of our situation; we live from moment to moment in a vast ocean of experience. In every instant, countless phenomena are arising and passing away—light, color, sound, flashes of thought, memory, and energy, flickers and shimmers and sparkles of sensation and feeling along with a host of other experiential phenomena for which there is no language.

Tim: But recognizing all the other things happening in the experiential field besides the whirlpools of emotional or physical pain doesn't make the pain go away, does it?

John: No, the whirlpool is still there, as part of the vast and boundless sea. But now you've awakened to its larger context, a context that we could say is infinite in its depth and scope. Of course, because the mind orients to the parts of the experiential field that it deems more important or meaningful, it may at times feel as if the difficult state being experienced is still overwhelming. But what begins to dawn is that relative to everything else showing up in the experiential field, any particular mental, emotional, or bodily state we might be encountering is still quite small, really infinitesimally so, in relation to the full field of experience.

         And so yes, painful situations and circumstances can be there and we do whatever we can to address them. But even as we do what we are able to most gracefully and skillfully navigate the turbulent waters that visit us, we can also explore what those whirlpools of experience are actually made of *and* open ourselves to the vast oceanic contexts within which those swirling currents exist.

Relaxing All Effort

Many, if not most, contemplative practices are defined by at least some measure of effort, some attempt at control, even if barely perceptible, some striving, even subtly, to arrive some place other than where we presently find ourselves, experientially. Otherwise, why even meditate in the first place? Why do anything we might call meditating or inquiring unless we believe at some level that where we currently find ourselves is somehow needing to be made better, enhanced, transformed, or even simply noticed?

With that in mind, here is a meditative approach you might enjoy experimenting with. You can listen to a recording of it at http://www.newharbinger.com/41818.

PRACTICE

Relax all effort to arrive somewhere else.

Relax all effort to define what you are.

Relax all effort to figure out what anything is.

Relax all effort to control what's here.

Relax all effort to make something else happen.

Relax all effort to keep anything from happening.

Relax all effort to direct the flow of attention.

Relax all effort to control the flow of anything.

Relax all effort to change what's here.

Relax all effort to keep what's here from changing.

And now, relax all effort to relax, and simply be…

Don't Do Anything About This

Generally speaking, we tend to believe that something must be done about what we're experiencing. To give but a few examples, we think we must find ways to make it less painful or more fulfilling, to understand why it's occurring, or to somehow manage or control it.

Now if you've had any exposure to practices such as meditation, you've undoubtedly been invited to enter into a different, less unconscious, less controlling, less judgmental relationship to your experience. Yet while such ways of interfacing with experience can no doubt be illuminating, there remains in such instructions an underlying belief that something *still* must be done about whatever is arising experientially—you have to notice it, remain aware of it, stay open to it, clarify its nature, let go of struggling with it, witness it, keep track of it, accept it, or allow it.

But maybe there's another option. Maybe you can experiment with *doing absolutely nothing* about experience other than letting it be enough. You can listen to a recording of the following practice at http://www. newharbinger.com/41818.

PRACTICE

For now, consider that there's no need to try to engage with or relate to or interface with experience in any particular way. There's no need to try to understand or explain it. No need to elaborate upon it. No need to try to fix it. No need to keep track of it. No need to try to control it. No need to obtain pleasure or meaning from it. No need to figure out where it came from or anticipate where it might go.

For now, let it be completely okay to not do anything about whatever may be appearing—no need to notice it, remain mindfully aware of it, describe it, accept it, or whatever you imagine ought to be done.

As you experiment in this way, I invite you to consider something quite remarkable—the experience you think you are remaining aware of, accepting, understanding, or making sense of? It has already vanished! Experience is *that* transient, that impermanent, that dynamic. And so, whatever experiences you imagine you are doing something about are actually no longer even here to do something about!

For now, instead of doing something about the experiences that are appearing, simply let them appear, which they are doing anyway, with or without your consent! Just let the fact of their appearance be enough. That's all.

Things appear and are complete and full in their very appearance and subsequent disappearance. And so nothing need be done about them; phenomena appear and dissolve spontaneously and effortlessly. This is the magical, miraculous, inexplicable display of reality.

Refer to Nothing

Even if this is all a dream or we are characters in someone's virtual reality game, something is undeniably present here. For simplicity, let's call this *experience*.

Now over the course of our lifetime, we have acquired not merely a host of ideas but a fairly sturdy conviction about what experiences are, as evidenced by the countless ways we have come to name and define whatever we encounter experientially.

Our capacity to build this seemingly secure base of knowledge about the world and ourselves rests in many ways upon the miracle of memory, this capacity consciousness has to refer back to previous experiential moments as a way of making sense of and characterizing, via language and concepts, what is presently arising. In short, when we encounter something, we essentially refer back, even if unconsciously, to what we have been taught via parents, friends, teachers, and the culture—what the phenomenon is, what it means, why it is arising, whether it is something to be sought after or avoided and so on.

As useful as it is to refer back to some idea or theory we may have about what we're experiencing, it can also be illuminating to let all of that prior knowledge fade into the background for a moment and in so doing, allow the vitality of whatever is present here to speak to us directly, in its *own* voice, on its own terms, unmediated by whatever we might think it is. Try out the following practice, or download a recording of it at http://www. newharbinger.com/41818.

PRACTICE

Right now, see what it's like not to refer or defer to any prior understanding, knowledge, belief, or theory you may have regarding what reality is or why it might be happening.

All the meaning-making frameworks you've ever been taught or adopted—"I'm a human being, trying to live by the principles I've been taught; I'm a little vulnerable primate running around attempting to stay safe on this rock flying through the vast expanse of space; I'm a meditator in search of greater peace and enlightenment; I'm a socially conscious being trying to create a saner, more humane and loving world…"

Whatever they may be, just let all of these ideologies, all these cosmologies, all these frames of reference fall away, if even for a brief moment...

See what it is like not to try to make sense of the moment by referring back to what you may have been told about it, whether from parents, religion, science, or culture.

Instead, just see what it is like to meet the reality of whatever is present here, on its own terms, without reference to any prior beliefs you may have about it.

What is this that is here? Feel the reality of what's present, without referencing memory to tell you what it is, without referring to any notions you may have about it.

The Continuous Discontinuity

We search for love, for happiness, for well-being, for peace. At times, we feel as if we've found whatever it is we're aspiring to realize, experiencing a moment where all seems unimaginably well, a moment of great vitality, happiness, or ease. And then it slips away, doesn't it? For this is the nature of experience, to disappear no sooner than it has appeared. Experiences always come. And they always go. It's unavoidable. The waves of perception are temporary, rising up and then returning from whence they came, only to be replaced by the next perceptual wave that appears.

And no matter how hard we may try to sustain those states that we typically equate with happiness and peace, we're simply unable to do so. At every turn, we find ourselves faced with the stark reality that despite our best efforts to obtain and then hold in place our positive states of mind, we are powerless to realize any kind of actual permanence or continuity because discontinuity is all there is. The river of experience never holds still. There are no frozen frames in the movie that is life, even if language gives us the impression that there are discrete moments with clear beginnings and ends. Life never remains the same but is always on the move.

Now conventionally we equate well-being with particular types of experience. We believe that happiness is dependent upon the flow of life looking a certain way ("comfortable," "happy") and imagine that when it appears differently ("uncomfortable" and "unhappy"), well-being is somehow absent. But what if there is another order of well-being altogether, one discovered not in the usual way we label our experiences, but rather in the flow of experiencing itself? What if well-being could be found not in particular, seemingly discrete perceptual states that are by nature fleeting, but in the continuous flow of perceiving itself, a flow that is by its very nature uninterrupted?

PRACTICE

For these next few moments, make no effort to try to manage or manipulate the flow of experiencing; simply relax the habit of trying to control the movement of life—twisting it into particular perceptual states you imagine will bring greater happiness.

Instead, let yourself discover that regardless of how the mind might be describing it, the river of experiencing flows continuously and effortlessly and is, by its very nature, at ease. Ever-changing, yet without interruption, a continuous discontinuity, a never-ending stream.

Mindfulness Is Unavoidable

In spiritual teachings and more recently the field of psychology, the distinction is made between moments of mindfulness and moments of unmindfulness. However, this turns out to be a misleading distinction, for with the possible exception of moments of deep, dreamless sleep or anesthesia, there really is no such thing as a moment without some degree of mindfulness or awareness present. Let's explore this...

PRACTICE

Students of meditation will typically be given some object to focus attention on, say the breath. The instruction will be to maintain focus there, to remain present with, say, the sensations of the breath. However, as every meditator knows, what invariably happens is that attention tends not to hold still but instead dances around, eventually moving away from the intended object and becoming engaged with some other aspect of experience such as the stream of thinking or imagining. The practitioner is then instructed, once he or she realizes awareness has been temporarily interrupted, to return to the original object of attention.

However, consider the following question: Is mindfulness or awareness ever really lost or diminished? Would it even be possible to know that we'd suffered some moment of so-called inattention, some lack of mindfulness, were mindfulness or awareness in fact absent?

How could we possibly know we'd been unaware without awareness being present in that moment to know the experience characterized as "being unaware"? How could we possibly know we'd failed to be present for much of a given meditation session, lost in a whirlpool of thinking, worrying, planning, or whatever, without mindfulness being present at least to some degree to register the supposed lack of mindfulness and the presence of thinking, worrying, and so on?

Are you in fact ever truly lost or entirely absent from the moments of your life?

Are you actually ever completely caught up in or distracted by some current of thinking or fantasizing such that there is no awareness that is even occurring? Or is some awareness always present, a mode of consciousness that is never completely absent and as a result, is able to report on its own purported absence?

Given what I'm suggesting here—that mindfulness or awareness is never actually absent—rather than practicing to find or develop more of something that we already naturally possess in spades, we can allow whatever practice we engage in to be an appreciation of the fact that mindfulness or awareness can never actually be lost because it constitutes the unavoidable reality underlying *all* moments of experiencing.

No matter how experience may appear and subsequently be characterized—clear, confused, dull, bright, aware, unaware—the very fact of its appearance is, you could say, the proof of mindfulness and its ever-present nature.

Sitting on a Chair Isn't Merely Sitting on a Chair

If someone were to contact you right now and ask what you were up to, you'd probably say something along the lines of, "I'm sitting here on a chair (or couch or bed), reading this book and experimenting with a meditation practice." It's a simple, straightforward and perfectly useful and reasonable way of categorizing or conveying what's happening experientially. But let's look a little more carefully at what is *actually* happening, beneath the surface of this conventional description.

PRACTICE

As you sit here, let yourself feel the actuality that "sitting on a chair meditating" is referring to. It's a concept, right? The question is: What is that concept pointing to in direct experience?

What's actually happening here that we then describe as sitting on a chair?

Allow yourself to explore the rich textures and subtleties of energy moving and dancing as this experience called "sitting on a chair." Just fall into whatever is here, feeling and being touched by what's present, noticing that the way you are characterizing this moment conceptually conveys almost nothing of the depth and detail that is actually present.

Let yourself enter into the depths of whatever experiential qualities are being felt and sensed right now. Something is here. Just feel the presence of that, much as you would feel the summer breeze as it caresses your skin or the warmth of the sun upon your face.

Now notice how your description of what's happening in any given moment can never encapsulate the inconceivable richness and fullness that is present. A simple phrase—sitting on a chair meditating—contains universes upon universes of sparkling, shimmering vitality and dynamism.

See that sitting on a chair meditating is just sitting on chair meditating and at the same time, so much more than that...

Let Yourself Be Astounded

Despite how amazing it is that anything even exists, we often take this simple fact for granted. Light, color, sound, touch, thought, feeling, sensation—we are so accustomed to the dazzling array of experiences bombarding us moment to moment that we often seem to lose sight of the astounding nature of everything, numb to just how remarkable, how miraculous, how inexplicable it all actually is.

PRACTICE

As you sit here, just let yourself be stunned by life, stupefied by the intelligence that is everywhere:

the functioning of billions of neurons strung together in a network of galactic proportions,

the unthinkable complexity of cellular metabolism,

the intricacy of the immune system,

the circulatory mechanisms that allow for the delivery of nutrients and oxygen to the body's tissues and organs,

and the capacity to create and understand language, to form thoughts and concepts, to hear sound, see light, to feel the infinitely subtle, multidimensional array of textures that present themselves every instant.

And all of it happening without a single thought or intention to make it so!

Drink in the mystery and inconceivability of it all; stand in awe of this awesomeness that is everywhere, the power, the presence, the vitality and dynamism that is appearing as every single flash instant of experiencing.

Revel in this miraculous, inexplicable presence, the intricacy and complexity and inconceivable functionality of everything, all of it utterly beyond the realm or reach of human comprehension.

Dialogue: *The Room*

Michelle: I find myself experiencing moments of greater openness, clarity, and ease, but it feels like I lose touch with those moments so easily. However, whenever we have our sessions here in this room, it's as if those feelings return and I'm able to reconnect with this sense of greater openness, presence, and ease.

John: No matter how wonderful a given "room" of experience may seem, we can't stay there. We'll be cast out of every one of those experience-rooms, however much we like them. Why? Because that's the nature of experience, to ceaselessly transform itself into something else.

   Of course, not only do we try to remain in the rooms that we like, but we try to leave the experience-rooms that we don't like and find ones that we imagine will be more satisfying. But as we know all too well, things frequently don't cooperate with or conform to the way we wish they would be!

   And yet, we have another choice: instead of constantly seeking to be in certain experiential rooms and avoid others, we can discover something that is present in *every* room of experience we may encounter.

Michelle: What do you mean?

John: Well, at the level of our descriptions, clearly no two rooms are alike. Every experience is utterly unique—pain is not pleasure; white is not black; happiness is not sorrow. But all experiences have one thing in common: their sheer presence. However we categorize it, experience may be many different things but it is always here, always simply present. And that is the common denominator of everything—its presence.

Michelle: Yes, but I find that when we meditate together during our sessions, that presence seems to come alive. I feel more aware, more awake, more in touch with just how amazing and miraculous the moment actually is, as you're fond of saying.

John: It can certainly seem that way. But actually, we're *always* meditating.

Michelle: How so?

John: Well, there may be many ways to conceive of what meditation is, but fundamentally, meditation is about being awake to what's here. And there is nothing *but* that.

Michelle: Nothing but meditation? Nothing but being awake? I don't understand.

John: All that is ever happening is experience, even though we can describe its tone and texture in a thousand different ways. While the moment might feel and be described as dull, uninteresting, or unpleasant, we can only ever experience and know we are experiencing these less than desirable qualities *because we are awake to them.* Meditation is often talked about in terms of being more present to *what is.* But presence is all there ever is! Whether we like them or not, experiences are, by definition, *always* present. And so from this vantage, meditation or presence is the continuous, uninterrupted state of affairs.

Michelle: So, why even meditate then?

John: Good question! Meditation, as it tends to be taught and understood, can bring a variety of benefits. But in my view, the supreme benefit and purpose of meditating is to recognize that meditation isn't necessary because we're always already doing it. Paying attention and noticing experience is the only thing that's ever actually happening.

Michelle: But are you denying that some experiences are more (or less) enjoyable, fulfilling, and inspiring than others? That certainly seems to be the case, at least to me.

John: At the level of description, all experiences are unique and distinctive. In any given moment the sense of being fulfilled is not the same as the feeling that we are somehow lacking. However, the way we define experiences is not the whole story. Let's take something neutral that we're all familiar with, the touch of our hand on skin. For the next few moments, place the palm of one hand on the top of the other hand. Just *feel* or *sense* what's there. What does the touch of your skin actually feel like?

Michelle: Well, it feels like the touch of my skin.

John: Fair enough. The sensation of touch has its own distinctive quality. We know it, which is how we're able to call it by name. But what is it, *really*? What *is* that particular texture we call "touch?" Feel the presence of it, the felt sense of your one hand on the other. Notice the dynamic nature of what's being sensed. Dive into whatever is present there, experientially. Submerge yourself in the complex kaleidoscope of sensations we call touch and ask yourself, what is this experience *actually* composed of?

We tend to take for granted that we know what an experience is simply because we have a name for it and can identify it as something distinct from other things. And yet, we can't quite put it into words, can we?

Even though we have a name for it, we can't definitively say, what touch is because it contains such an array of experiential qualities, a universe of indescribable nuance, subtlety, and depth. Touch is simply touch. And yet it's also so much more than that label can convey. The experience we call touch is actually an endless free fall into mystery. But what's so remarkable and liberating about all of this is that it doesn't apply merely to touch but is the hallmark of *everything* that is experienced.

Michelle: What do you mean when you say that it's liberating?

John: We might define certain experiences as desirable or undesirable, fulfilling or unfulfilling, captivating or boring. But if we stop for a moment and simply feel what is present, we'll discover, just as we did with the sensations of touch, that regardless of what we imagine things to be, experiences cannot be definitively described because they're infinitely complex and continuously changing.

Whether it's the sense of touching or being touched, a sound, a feeling, or a visual image, the reality is that experience appears without any labels. The definitions, the conceptual categories, the linguistic descriptions...these are all superimposed on a reality that is undefined. The myriad narratives we entertain, as compelling as these may be, are not intrinsic to experience. They are imagined, defined into existence.

Michelle: I don't understand. Let's say I experience an uncomfortable mental-emotional state and find it difficult to get myself unstuck from it. Are you telling me the emotion and the feeling of being stuck in it are not actually present, but merely imagined?

John: Yes, that's precisely what I'm suggesting. When we explored the example of touch, we found that what seems relatively easy to identify and categorize is in fact an indefinable mystery. At one level, it's experienced as something structured, coherent, and definable. But when we attempt to locate some definite structure or coherence, we come up empty-handed. What seemed to be something definite turns out to be beyond any possibility of being defined. And so, we can explore any experience we imagine to be a problem, a source of bondage or limitation, and discover that that very experience is, by its nature, utterly free, unbound, and unlimited.

While it may seem as if we're moving in and out of various rooms, consider this: we really live inside a single room, the room of experiencing. There is no entering or exiting this room but only the constant changing and shifting of whatever we might find there.

Let the Winds Blow

Sometimes (maybe even often) the mind can feel like quite the hurricane. Now, many teachings encourage the aspirant to employ all manner of strategies to make that restlessness and commotion settle down, to find a place of calm and rest somewhere, apart from or beyond the tumult. It's understandable that we'd be drawn to follow such guidance and engage in different practices to go from a state of noise and unrest to one that is quieter and more peaceful. But look at the universe itself, of which we are obviously a part—stars exploding, galaxies expanding, meteors colliding, storms erupting—it isn't really a quiet or peaceful place, is it? Given this, could it be that the effort to calm all this wild activity down is a fool's errand?

However beneficial it may be to try to calm the turbulence that often visits us, there is another choice, one that requires no effort, and that is to simply let the hurricanes rage and in that discover that those oftentimes ferocious mental-emotional winds may not be the problem we imagine them to be.

PRACTICE

For these next moments, simply allow the winds of experience to blow, however they wish to blow. Whether a gentle breeze or a powerful gale force, make no effort to control the winds of life surging within, around, and as you.

No need to try to stand apart from the swirling energies of thought, feeling, and sensation to find some sanctuary of peace. You can't really separate yourself from experience anyway!

Just let go of applying any effort to try to manage the winds.

You'll begin to discover that all that dynamic energy and oftentimes chaotic, unpredictable movement was never actually the problem you imagined it to be. It's just the nature of life to be that alive, to spin and whirl and dance with complete freedom and abandon, uncontained and explosive.

Life is never at war with itself, but only ever at ease and at rest with even its fiercest expressions, for it *is* those very expressions, as are you.

Boundaries

Most of us take for granted that we are bounded creatures, that there is a clear point where "we" come to an end and the world outside of us begins. However, let's explore this whole question, investigating our own direct experience to see if we can actually find any direct evidence to support the substantiality of these apparent boundaries we've come to believe in so unquestioningly. You can listen to a recording of it at http://www.newharbinger.com/41818.

PRACTICE

Look and see if you can locate a line, something demarcating what you call self from not-self. Can any clear boundary be found?

"Well," you might say, "yes, my skin separates me from the world."

Okay, but let's examine that apparent boundary.

Feel into the experience of what you call "skin"—is there an actual edge to it? Can you identify where the skin comes to an end and the world on the other side of that skin line begins? It's blurry, isn't it, this supposed distinction between inside and outside, this borderline we imagine exists between self and other?

If you find what you believe to be some clearly identifiable boundary line, something separating inner from outer, explore the specific details of this apparent dividing line.

Ask yourself, "Can I find the edge of it? Can I locate specifically where this purported boundary comes to an end?" Feel into the existence of this presumed border—what do you find there, not as an idea of something that must be separating one thing from another, but as an actuality? Can any real, discernible line be found?

Now let's explore another boundary, the one we imagine exists between past, present, and future.

Look very carefully and sensitively at your experience—can you identify the precise instant when this moment comes to an end and what we might call "the future" begins? Can you find any clear demarcation there?

If such a division actually exists, you ought to be able to locate it, right? If it's real, it should be findable, this line we imagine is separating one moment from the next.

But can any such line or demarcation be found? Where, if anywhere, does this moment end and the next begin? Look not to your concepts to answer this question but to your direct experience... What do you find there?

Finally, let's examine one more supposed boundary, the one between the perceiver and the perceived.

With eyes open, look at some object in your field of vision, maybe the view of a tree or flower outside your window.

Conventionally, we would regard the tree or flower as an object that's being perceived by us, the perceiving subject. But let's have a closer look at that presumed distinction between what's perceiving and whatever is being perceived. To be sure, we imagine there exists and might even argue that we experience an actual line separating us from whatever it is that's being seen, heard, tasted, or touched. But again, let's examine that presumed separation.

Take the object you've chosen; whatever it is, simply look at it. See how it appears. Notice that as much as this object seems to be "out there," existing outside of yourself, it's impossible to tell where you as the perceiver end and the object being perceived begins.

Conventionally, we may make a clear distinction between whatever is being seen and the one who is seeing. But look again...

Can any such line be found? Can you locate the place where you as perceiver come to a stop and the object being perceived begins? Or is there only a seamless flow of perceiving occurring?

Notice the paradoxical nature of all of this, that the perceiver and perceived co-arise, appearing as a singular, undivided whole with no clear boundary line separating one from the other.

And yet despite this inability to locate any clear border or boundary, the perceiver and perceived, the subjective and objective poles of experience appear to us as distinct and separate. While this paradox may seem contradictory to the reasoning mind, it is nevertheless our direct experience, a world of apparent subjects and objects that appear recognizable and distinct from one another while at the same time no clear lines of division are anywhere to be found.

Reality: *Virtual, Actual...or Both?*

As we look not merely at the ideas we hold about things ("that's a tree, a computer, a joy, a sadness...") but at their sheer actuality, the raw, felt sense or presence of whatever is being perceived, it begins to dawn on us just how impossible it is to capture or convey things linguistically. What appears in the field of experience is beyond any and all descriptions or conceptualizations, even if aspects of language are able to hint at the myriad qualitative and textural dimensions of things.

What I'm suggesting is that the way the world is conventionally seen and understood is itself an abstraction—we have, in effect, been living in and relating to a kind of virtual world, a conceptualization of experience rather than its actuality. This conventional, consensus reality says, "the wind is blowing on my face." But in truth, each of the dimensions of this familiar experience—wind, blowing, face—all contain inconceivable perceptual and sensorial universes within them. Put another way, what is a face, the wind, or the activity of blowing, beyond the mere concepts used to characterize or label such phenomena? Let's explore just one of these aspects, the face.

PRACTICE

As you sit here, I invite you to close your eyes and simply feel your face. Notice the rich array of experiential phenomena that are present; immerse yourself in whatever is there, whatever it is that constitutes this reality you call your face. It's astounding how much is actually present—flashes and flickers of energy, shimmers of sensation, deep dark canyons of subtle phenomena for which there really are no words.

Of course, the mind's job is to reduce all of this unthinkably rich complexity, depth, and detail into a single word or concept. But just notice what an impossible task that actually is. Feel the worlds upon worlds of experience contained in this one body part we call the face.

Now there's no need to negate the mind's labeling and describing of things. It's not actually a problem, plus you can't really turn that automatic process off anyway! But it is possible to see that the mind's conceptual rendering of things is just one way of experiencing reality. As we've been exploring, there's another way to encounter things, one that doesn't merely collapse the apparent patterns of life into fixed categories or mental frameworks, but instead recognizes that the vast, unbounded nature of every momentary perception cannot, in the end, be convincingly reduced or collapsed into *any* definition.

The simplest way to discover what I am pointing to here is to just *feel* whatever is present. That's it. To be sure, reality is being thought about or conceived. And that is totally fine. But experiences are also being known or felt, nonconceptually. Simply feeling what is present here and how it transcends our notions about what it is reveals just how astonishing and ultimately unfathomable reality actually is.

Everything Is Present

Our attention is typically focused on the qualitative differences we encounter in life—that's hot, that's cold, that's easy, that's difficult, that's clarifying, that's confusing, that's exciting, that's boring, that's comfortable, that's uncomfortable, and so on. But, however natural it may be for us to do this, an unintended consequence is that we end up expending considerable effort trying to secure more of the moments we equate with our definitions of happiness and avoid or escape those we imagine will keep us from it. Unfortunately, we're frequently unable to create or to hold in place the moments we consider positive or keep at bay those we deem negative or undesirable. But there's an alternative to this all too familiar dynamic...

PRACTICE

For these next few moments, rather than emphasizing the particular content or flavor of experience, simply feel the presence of it. If what you label as comfort is there, feel the presence of that. If discomfort is what's arising, then feel its presence.

There's no need to favor one thing over another.

Quiet mind? That's what is present.

Busy mind? Then that is what's present.

A sense of unease? Present.

A sense of feeling unbounded and free? Present.

See the bird in the tree? Present.

Hear the roar of traffic outside? Present.

Feel as if you're somehow not getting this? No problem—that is just what's present! See, there's no doing this right, there is simply what's present. And that can never be lost, even if what's present is forever slipping away, becoming the next thing that is present...

For these next few moments, instead of emphasizing how things are appearing, just notice the fact that they even *are* appearing, the simple but astounding reality of their presence. It doesn't matter how the moment is showing up; simply notice that it is showing up, that it is present and that this presence is continuous, even if its permutations are forever changing.

See that you never have to bring yourself back to presence because wherever you may venture within the vast field of experience, presence announces its presence as that very experience.

Presence need not be achieved or practiced but simply noticed as the unavoidable reality of every instant. And should you feel as if you have somehow failed to notice this, well, then that's exactly what will be present!

The Phenomenal Nature of Phenomena

If you have ever attempted to sit quietly and do absolutely nothing for some extended period of time, what is sometimes called "meditation," you may have discovered an interesting thing. In such moments, even without any external demands being placed upon you to do or solve or fix anything, you can often feel as if there is still something not quite right or okay about whatever is being experienced.

In response to this sense that something is out of place, our impulse is to try to do something about whatever we imagine is wrong or problematic so as to improve upon the moment's apparent lack or insufficiency. This sense that something is not quite right about what's appearing experientially and our efforts to then fix that apparent problem can take many forms—feeling as if we should be experiencing something more fulfilling or exciting, that we should be more mindful or aware, that we should be experiencing less distraction, less agitation, more ease, less thinking, more acceptance. And on and on it goes...

But maybe the only thing that makes an experience into an apparent problem we must solve is viewing it as such. Could it be that we literally define problems into existence by virtue of the ways we frame or interpret them? Let's explore this, experimenting with the possibility that from a certain perspective, there are no problems but only experiences.

PRACTICE

For the next few moments, there's only one thing to do: don't make anything you might be experiencing into a problem. Even if you notice yourself turning experience into something you think must be fixed or resolved, let that not be a problem either.

In this meditation, let nothing, and I mean absolutely nothing, be a problem, including the belief that something is a problem!

Struggling with experience? No problem.

Feeling at ease with experience? No problem.

Experiencing states conventionally labeled as positive? No problem.

Being visited by so-called negative states? No problem.

Quiet mind? No problem.

Restless mind? No problem.

Feeling that no experience is ever a problem? No problem.

Thinking some experiences are problems? No problem!

Let no experience be wrong or out of place; let no moment be anything other than the perfect, inescapable expression of life that it is in the instant of its arising.

Personal growth "technologies" (be they self-help, psychological, or spiritual in nature) are typically aimed at eliciting certain experiences, experiences imagined to be more important or special than the ones presently occurring. However, the most interesting and liberating approaches are those that reveal the profundity and specialness of *all* experience.

It's fair to say that the fact that experience is occurring at all is the greatest, most stupefying of miracles. And yet the only thing that keeps us from recognizing the extraordinary, remarkable nature of every momentary perception is the way in which we define and limit phenomena that are by nature indefinable and unlimited. The reality is that *every* moment of experience, regardless of its conventional descriptive label, is an inconceivably rich and profound expression of crackling, sizzling, dynamic energy and intelligence.

Behold the phenomenal nature of all phenomena, even the ones we conventionally label as problems!

The Mystery of Intention

Our seeming capacity for agency, this conviction that we're capable of making free choices, of exercising our intention and self-will is, by and large, completely taken for granted by most of us. However, a careful investigation into these conventional assumptions reveals the entire question of free will and our apparent ability to exercise choice and intentionality as far from being resolved. Let's have a look…

PRACTICE

In a moment, I'm going to invite you to choose some simple activity, and then ask you to carry that out. It doesn't matter what you end up selecting; it could be anything really, maybe moving your hand a certain way, opening or closing your eyes, stretching your body, standing up, or thinking about something. Again, the choice you make is not what's important. You'll simply decide to do *something* and then do whatever it is you've intended to do. That's it!

First, before you decide, pay very careful attention to your field of experience. Just let yourself be aware of whatever is here experientially, feeling the raw presence of it.

Now, go ahead and choose your intended action, and then carry it out.

Considering your original intention, which you believe was freely chosen and initiated by you, ask yourself: Where did that intention actually come from?

Are you able to find its beginning, the origin or source of it? How was it that you happened to choose the action that you did?

Whether it was to move your arm, stretch your legs, open your eyes, or whatever, from where did the impetus to do that emerge?

Out of the virtually infinite number of possible actions you could have taken, how was it that you happened to choose the one that you did?

Look very carefully: What led to or initiated the choice that you made?

Can you identify the genesis of it?

Was it a thought that began it all and if so, how was is that that particular thought and not some other arose? Did you really choose to have the thought to do whatever you did?

Right now, you are reading this book and you probably believe that you freely chose to read it at this particular time. But consider this: Where did that decision to read at this moment actually come from?

This most familiar and taken-for-granted of human experiences—the feeling as if it is *we* who are the agents of whatever we've chosen or intended to do—turns out upon closer examination to be a vast, fathomless mystery, impossible to locate, impossible to pinpoint, impossible to grasp hold of or define.

Not Privileging Thought

Whenever we find ourselves caught up in some painful web of thinking, countless other phenomena are also being experienced—the blue of the sky; the dust on the windowsill; the sound of wind in the trees. However, our tendency is to view these other phenomena as somehow less consequential or maybe even completely insignificant compared with the uncomfortable thoughts that sometimes visit us.

And yet, this privileging of thinking over other modes of experiencing such as hearing, seeing, feeling, or sensing is completely arbitrary. In any moment that we might find ourselves thinking about something that's occurred or has yet to occur, sounds are still appearing, light is still present, colors are still exploding all around us, and untold sensations are still arising. Could it be that these other aspects of experience, none of which have anything to do with the mental narratives going on, are of equal value and import?

You can download a recording of the practice below at http://www.newharbinger.com/41818.

PRACTICE

For the next few moments, place no greater weight or significance upon the movement of thought than you would any other dimension of experience.

That little itch you're feeling on your arm? Equally as relevant as the most sublime or most disturbing thought that might arise.

The sounds of traffic outside? As full of meaning as any thought that might be appearing.

The subtle presence of sensations and feelings in the body? No less important than whatever you might be thinking right now.

For now, just put thinking in its proper place, on equal footing with everything else being experienced, recognizing that thought does not merit more attention or devotion than anything else for everything is equal: equal in its importance, equal in its richness and meaningfulness, equal in its miraculous, unfathomable vitality and presence.

Let your attention be wide open, noticing not merely the waves of thought but also the countless other phenomena that make up the vast and boundless sea of experience.

What's True About This?

We've learned so much from others—parents, friends, teachers, our community, science, religion—we've been taught how to make sense of it all, how to understand and interpret what's here, what experience is, who we are, what life is, and what it all might mean. But what if instead of deferring to what others have told us about what the reality of experiencing is, we simply let *experience itself* tell us what it is? The practice below gives you a tool for directly experiencing this. You can download a recording of it at http://www.newharbinger.com/41818.

PRACTICE

For these next few moments, simply let all the knowledge you've accumulated about the world recede into the background, meeting what is here freshly, without any presuppositions about what it might be or mean.

You may have a hundred different thoughts about what's happening right now.

But for these next few moments, just let all of that fade away and simply feel the nature and presence of whatever is here, beyond what anyone else may have told you about it.

Allow yourself to be touched by the actuality of whatever is showing up in experience.

Rather than you telling experience what it is using the many labels and definitions you've learned along the way, simply let experience itself tell you what it is, speaking to you in its own unfathomable yet ever-present language.

This Is It

If I had to sum up the central theme of this book, I would do so with the following phrase: "This Is It." Let me unpack those three powerful words…

"This" refers to whatever is showing up right now, whatever is being seen, heard, noticed, experienced…This.

"Is" refers to the presence of This, to the simple, undeniable fact that This exists right now, that This *Is*.

Finally, "It" points to the reality that *This* is all there is. After all, what else could there ever be but This? It might be argued that there could be something other than This, at least hypothetically. But the only way to know that for sure would be to have some experience of that other something. And once we have an experience of that *something else*, it ceases to be something else and becomes This! In other words, anything other than This could only ever exist as an abstraction.

PRACTICE

This Is It…let's explore these three simple words…

This, just This.

Whatever is arising, whatever is showing up, whatever is appearing spontaneously as the field of experience, just feel This. Feel the myriad ways This moves, the way This dances around, the way This changes from one instant to the next.

Feel how dynamic, how slippery, how ungraspable and ultimately indescribable This is.

Now simply appreciate that This Is, that This even exists. Feel the presence of This, the aliveness of This, the vitality of This, the actuality of This.

We cannot know for certain how or why This is here. But *that it is*, is undeniable.

Feel the miracle of that, the miracle that This Is.

And now, just appreciate that This Is It, that it's simply not possible for there to be anything *but* This.

This must be everything you could ever hope or dream of since there could never be anything but This.

In all its infinite variety, the untold ways it can be, *This Is Always It.*

Resting as the View

In some traditions, the practitioner is instructed to "rest in the view." The view refers to that which is aware of every fleeting instant and is often described as an unchanging stability, a vast and spacious clarity within which all experience arises and passes away.

Based on the way *the view* is often taught, we conceive of it as being something distinct from whatever is being viewed. However, if we think of the view as some privileged domain, some special state or realm we must first locate and then rest in, we will miss the fact that this very moment is *already* the view. To be sure, that which is being seen or viewed is forever changing. But the seeing itself is constant; something is *always* being experienced, *always* being felt, *always* being viewed...

And so to "rest as the view" is simply to see that there is *only* resting in the view, only ever the knowing of whatever is being known, the seeing of whatever is being seen, the feeling of whatever is being felt. This isn't about finding and then resting in the view but rather seeing that there is no possibility of ever being *out* of the view! Resting is not something we do; it is simply noticing that the view is inescapable, ever-present as *this* very instant...and the next.

PRACTICE

We needn't rest in the view so much as see that the view is already present, as each fleeting moment of experience. Nothing need be done to bring the view about. It is spontaneously present, with no effort required.

Whatever your gaze may happen to fall upon, know that right there is the view, the view of whatever is present. Rest effortlessly right here, here in the heart of this knowing, the steadfastness and constancy of the view.

Seeing something? That is the view.

Feeling something? That is the view.

Experiencing something? That is the view.

Thinking something? That is the view.

Feeling something? That is the view.

There is only the view, the view of whatever is appearing!

The Ease of Being Here

Many teachings advise the student to engage in various practices to become more aware of the present moment, awake to the here and now. But the funny thing about it is that what we call "the here and now" is spontaneously present as the only reality. Here is always here. Now is always now. Presence is always present, without any striving, doing, or meditating required.

Since here appears effortlessly, nothing need be done to create or sustain it. It is relentlessly present. Any apparent absence of it, any supposed loss of contact with the here and now is simply another of the here and now's countless and ceaseless manifestations.

What we call "losing contact with the present moment" is simply another present moment, another here and now. In other words, here is inescapable!

PRACTICE

For these next few moments, simply notice and appreciate the simple fact that here is already here, that now is always now, regardless of anything we might be doing to realize that.

Here remains here, no matter the form it may be taking. Here never departs from itself, even as it is constantly transforming into the next thing.

See that no matter what is arising, no matter what is being experienced, here is here.

No effort is ever required for this to be true.

No doing is needed to make the miracle that is present be present.

See that you are powerless to make this here and now disappear.

The Miracle of Perceiving

As humans, we long to experience a sense of fulfillment that we can count on, that is stable and reliable, a well-being and happiness that is not constantly coming and going. And while we imagine this enduring well-being will somehow be found in particular types of experiences or circumstances, the problem is that no experiential pattern ever endures. And so, our efforts to secure any sort of lasting well-being in phenomena that are by nature unstable and impermanent are doomed to fail.

The undeniable reality is that every experience is here for a brief instant and then it vanishes, giving way to something else. What is being seen, heard, and felt is in a state of constant flux. This is the dynamic, non-static nature of everything.

Given the impermanence of experience, the natural question arises: Is there anything that will bring us constancy or stability? The answer is "yes." For while experiences come and go, *experiencing* itself does not. The flow of experiencing is ongoing. It is the sole constant. To be sure, perceptions are forever changing. But the perceiving itself never stops. You can download a recording for this chapter at http://www.newharbinger. com/41818.

PRACTICE

While our tendency to emphasize the content of our inner or outer weather—is it cold or hot, sunny or cloudy, stormy or calm?—is quite normal and natural, for the next few moments, I invite you into another experiment.

Rather than orienting to the content of whatever is being experienced, how it feels, what it sounds like, the particular shape, color, and texture of it, simply appreciate the fact that experiencing is even happening at all.

Notice that something is here, something is present, something is being perceived. But don't worry about what that something is or how it is being labeled or described.

Instead, just revel in the fact that it is even here.

Let your emphasis be on the fact that something is present rather than trying to figure out what that something is, which really can't be done anyway! While the experiences are impermanent, here and then gone in a flash, notice that the flow of experiencing itself never comes to a stop.

Feel its constancy, the relentlessness of experiencing, how it never turns off, even if the content of it is forever in flux.

See that nothing need be done, that no effort is required to make the flow of experiencing constant, for that is its nature, never to cease.

Marvel at its presence; let yourself be astounded by it, this miraculous light of experiencing that can never be switched off.

Expressions of Energy

A recurring theme throughout this book is the invitation to shift our emphasis from the content of experience, the labels, descriptions, conceptual interpretations of it, to the sheer presence or existence of it. One powerful way to get a sense of the liberating impact of this change in how we orient to experience is to feel each moment, no matter how we might be characterizing it—fear, sorrow, joy, anger, elation—as an expression or manifestation of a kind of basic, fundamental energy—the energy, we could say, of life itself.

PRACTICE

For these next few moments, imagine your thoughts, feelings, and sensations as different forms or expressions of life energy. If what you call joy is present, feel it as the movement of a kind of energy. If confusion or agitation is arising, see or feel that as energy. If peace or tranquility is present, then see those experiential textures as yet another form that the energy of life can take.

With your eyes open or closed, simply let all these energetic expressions move and dance and swirl, however they wish. Make no effort to alter, control, or direct the ceaseless unfolding of life's energetic flow.

Now see that you yourself—the one sitting here meditating—are yet another one of these energetic expressions, and simply allow this unfolding of energy that is you to move and dance and swirl, however it wishes.

Simply feel the raw presence of whatever is here. Listen to the ceaseless hum of being. You can't help but hear it for it is the sound of everything, being itself.

Hear the sound of traffic outside? That's it, the hum of being.

Hear the gurgling of your stomach or the beat of your heart? That's it too…the hum of being.

Hear the sound of thoughts racing through your mind? The hum of being…

For now, let it matter not what's appearing but simply appreciate and savor the fact that it is. Let yourself be awestruck that anything is even happening at all, that this existence, this presence, this energy and aliveness is appearing in all the wildly colorful, dynamic, and unpredictable ways that it does.

We Have Not Been Here Before

The conventional view is that there is a kind of stasis or regularity to things and experiences and that this stability defines our lives. We imagine that things are, for all intents and purposes, more or less the same from moment to moment. This is how the world of experiences and circumstances appears recognizable. Some mental-emotional state arises and we recognize that pattern; it feels familiar: "Oh yeah, I know what that is. It's fear...."

Similarly, we see some object or return to some place and recognize it as more or less the same object or place we'd previously visited: "Oh sure, that's my car or my house or my friend or the neighborhood I live in..."

However, true as it may seem that experiences and objects have a kind of persistence or continuity to them from moment to moment, that they are essentially what they were when we last encountered them, the fact is that they are not, at least not exactly. Your friend or that emotion you're being visited by may look, feel, or behave in such a way that makes it seem recognizable to you. But the fact is that we have *never* actually experienced this moment before. Yes, experiences appear and feel very familiar to us. But true as that sense of familiarity may be, the reality is that we've never actually felt this particular moment, at least not in this exact way. No experience, no moment, no person, place, or thing is ever quite the same owing to its radically dynamic, non-static, alive nature.

PRACTICE

Imagine being transported to another world, a planet that is utterly foreign to you. Not a single thing about this extraterrestrial world could possibly be familiar or known to you because you've never actually seen, felt, touched, or tasted any part of it before.

Now imagine your everyday experience to be this hypothetical foreign land. Whatever way you might conventionally describe what's happening—holding a glass of water in your hand, seeing a cloud-filled sky, hearing the sound of traffic on the street, feeling the wind upon your face—just go ahead and notice whatever is present here, traveling through this heretofore unseen world, exploring the remarkable experiential landscape that lies before you.

Since everything is new to you here, don't bother referring to any previously learned names or descriptors to make sense of what you're seeing because those categories no longer apply. You're literally in a different world now!

Just behold the infinite detail, depth, and dimensionality that is here, not one iota of which you have ever seen nor will you ever see again.

Let the truth of this sink in, this astounding fact that you cannot possibly know what this world is that you are experiencing right now, for one simple reason: you have never actually been here before!

Everything Slips Away

No matter how hard we may try, there's really no way to determine what this moment is. While we're constantly drawing conclusions about experience, we can't actually pull it off for as soon as we engage in some interpretation, the very thing we imagine we've defined has shifted into something else owing to its ever-changing, dynamic nature. The fact is that everything is in a state of constant, unstoppable flux and flow, incapable of being held in place, impossible to keep from vanishing and becoming the next instant, the next appearance… You can listen to a recording of the practice below at http://www.newharbinger.com/41818.

PRACTICE

For these next few moments, simply notice how everything slips away.

Thoughts appear and then vanish in an instant. Momentary eruptions of feeling arise and then dissolve, transforming themselves into the next thing. Sounds and sights emerge and then fade away. Like a river, experience is forever on the move, never holding still, always becoming something else. Thoughts, feelings, and sensations appear, then disappear in a single, indistinguishable movement, a dance of endless dynamism and unstoppable change.

Notice how it is simply not possible to hold anything in place, to keep what is from mutating.

We speak of trying to let go of what troubles us, but the reality is that letting go is already the nature of things. Nothing need be done to make this so. The release of things is effortless and spontaneous; it requires no doing for it is the unavoidable nature of everything to let go of itself, every instant.

Feel the reality of this. See how there can be no holding on to experience owing to its relentlessly transient nature, every moment slipping away, regardless of how we may try to orient ourselves to it.

Our experiences disappear of their own accord. We needn't do anything to bring this about.

With the perception you are having right now, just try to keep it in place, try to hold it here, see if you can stop it from morphing into the next experience. It cannot be done. Feel the wondrous freedom of this, the impossibility of ever holding on to anything.

The Knowing of This Moment Is the Feeling of It

Contemplative traditions the world over speak about awareness as that which is most central to human experience; without it, without this capacity to know, there would simply *be* no experience (see the chapter "What is Awareness?").

When pointing others to awareness, the argument frequently goes something like this: "How do you know you are having the experience of happiness or sadness? How do you know sounds are being heard, sights are being seen, or that you exist? You know these things because awareness is present. Awareness is the light that illumines everything, the light that makes everything known."

While this way of speaking of the knowing function of consciousness can be very powerful, for some people, the term "awareness" can at times come across as overly abstract and difficult to understand or grasp experientially.

So, here's another way to understand what awareness is—awareness is not merely that which illumines or makes things known, though it is certainly that. Awareness is also that which *feels* experience.

PRACTICE

Look in your experience right now and ask, "Are thoughts occurring in this moment?"

If they are, how is that fact being known? How is it that you can say thoughts are arising and be so certain of that? Well, thoughts, like everything else, have a certain distinctive texture, we could say. And it is that unique quality or texture that is being felt and which reveals the presence of this phenomenon we call "thought."

Are sounds being heard right now?

If you answer "yes," again, how do you know this? Well, because of the particular texture that constitutes sound and nothing else. And that distinctive textural quality is what is *felt* as this thing we call "sound."

Seeing light? How do you know that?

Again, it is because the experiential quality we call light is being felt. In other words, we know things *are* because they are felt. Awareness and feeling are really synonyms, for to be aware is to *feel* whatever appears. And so just as we might explore the miracle of awareness by inquiring into what it is that knows experience, we can also ask the question, what is it that *feels* the presence of anything and everything?

Here is a poem. Let it be a meditation on this miracle of feeling-awareness that brings each and every moment to life.

No matter how seemingly subtle or gross
here we are, feeling everything,
the light that shines upon the waking world
and the deepest darkness of our sleeping nights.
Whether roaring or barely heard,
here we are, feeling everything,
the music of the birds and swaying trees
and the songs of laughing, crying people everywhere.
Be it tangible or intangible
here we are, feeling everything,
the trillions of starlit thoughts flickering
inside the vast and borderless sky
and the rush of watery emotions
as they splash and surge upon our shores.
Whether obvious or hidden from view,
here we are, feeling everything,
the unfathomable mystery of it all,
the unknowable, inconceivable reality
shining forth as everything,
life feeling and knowing itself
as the intimacy of this.

Being Here Now

Ram Dass titled his iconic book *Be Here Now*, words that countless seekers, myself included, took as a kind of spiritual prescription or practice to take up. But as it turns out, rather than being a prescription, *be here now* is really a description of the way things actually are. In other words, there is nothing *but* being here now. There is only ever the presence of what is. Being. And that which is present is always present, always simply and effortlessly here and now. *Being here now* need not be cultivated or contrived but simply seen to be the sheer, unavoidable, ever-present fact of existence itself.

And while it is not necessary to practice *being here now* for it is already the case, this fact can, paradoxically, be discovered by engaging in what one might arguably call "practice." As I see it, meditation is a trick we can use to discover that meditation isn't actually necessary! So with that in mind, here's a meditative trick to play with. You can download a recording of it at http://www.newharbinger.com/41818.

PRACTICE

Notice that no matter where the mind might travel, no matter how seemingly far into the past or future we may appear to venture, it is absolutely, unequivocally impossible to exist in any time other than now.

There is no escaping the reality of this.

Notice how powerless we are to leave this moment. No matter what past or future time we might seem to wander off into, it always remains now, a now that is at the same time always new, always fresh, always remaking itself, forever on the move, becoming the next thing…

Now, see that no matter where you might travel off to in seeming space, you can never actually go anywhere for you remain forever in one place: here!

There is no escaping here, for whatever we might think of or call "there" could only ever be experienced *here*.

As with time, just let yourself notice this fact, that regardless of what lands you might venture off to, it is simply not possible to depart from here.

And so it turns out that here is not some "place" we must practice remaining in. Instead, we can simply notice that it is not possible to be anywhere *but* here! Here is the only place we can ever be.

Feel the reality of this, the astounding fact that here can never be taken away for it is literally all that exists.

There is no possibility of ever being removed from here because wherever we might be taken, one small step or to the farthest reaches of the universe and beyond, we always remain right here. And so we are, quite literally, always here and it is always now. This is the inescapable fact, the truth that no matter what lands we may venture off to, no matter what states we may enter or exit, what places we may visit and then depart from, we are forever being here now.

Presence

"Presence," a word we often hear in psychological and spiritual circles, tends to be spoken of as if it were some rarefied state distinct from other states and definitely not what we're currently experiencing! Presence tends to get framed as some special realm or dimension of consciousness that we must somehow locate, cultivate, practice, rest in, commit ourselves to, and so on. But rather than assuming this to be true, let's look to see if it is actually the case. You can listen to a recording of the following practice at http://www.newharbinger.com/41818.

PRACTICE

Consider the following: Has there ever been a time when presence was in fact absent or missing? Is that even possible? Hasn't something always been present? Hasn't something always been here?

Look and see if you have ever lost or been separate from presence.

Teachings may proclaim that such experiences as thinking or the sense of being a separate person somehow veil or keep us from realizing presence. But whether we call it "thinking" or "feeling a sense of separation," the presence of *any* experience is, by definition, still present.

The experiences we label as stuck, twisted up in knots, frustrated, lost, grasping, or annoyed are nothing but pure, unadulterated, sparklingly alive presence. The truth is that presence need not be sought or practiced for there is nothing *but* presence, even if that which is present is constantly changing from moment to moment.

Now while something is clearly present, notice that we cannot at the same time say precisely what that "something" is, since what's present is really beyond any and all definitions.

Try it right now. Feel what is here, experientially. Feel whatever is arising in this oh-so-fleeting moment. You may have many different names for it. But see that no conceptual labels apply, for whatever is present cannot be collapsed into any description or category.

Thinking? Sensing? Feeling? The seeing of light? The hearing of sounds? The deepest sorrow? The greatest joy?

While undeniably present, none of these labels is capable of adequately conveying the infinite, indefinable nature of what is actually here, the pure presence and utter mystery of this.

The most obvious quality of "this" that is present is that it is. Whatever is here, however we might conceive of it, is all pure vitality, pure aliveness. While the diverse forms, shapes, colors, and textures this can take are absolutely staggering, *that it even exists at all* seems the most astounding mystery and miracle. This is. Wow! How is that even possible? How is it that anything is actually present, that anything is?

Feel that. Whatever shape reality might be taking, feel the awesome power and vitality that is its very existence.

Feel the undeniable, inescapable and potent presence of presence, the here of here.

Notice that it's not presence on one side, knowing, watching, or being aware of something else "over there." No, it's *all* presence. No inside, no outside, no here nor there but simply this that is present. There isn't anything else. For after all, what else could there ever be? If something else were to appear, something else were to become known, it would still be just this presence.

Were we to become aware of some other dimension, some other realm or reality, we would still be right here, knowing and feeling the presence of this. We could travel to the farthest reaches of the cosmos, have the most mind-boggling transcendental otherworldly experiences and it would still be just this, this very presence.

Drifting Toward Reality

If you've ever practiced meditation, you very likely received guidance to focus on some aspect of experience, maybe the process of breathing or body sensations. When engaging in such practices, we quickly discover that attention tends to drift from one thing to the next. And when this inevitably occurs, one is typically instructed to keep track of this drifting of attention and whenever it is noticed, simply redirect the mind back to its chosen object.

In both psychology and spirituality, the wandering of attention is frequently portrayed as a problem we must work very diligently to overcome. However, as valid as that perspective might be in certain contexts, I invite you into another consideration: drifting is what experience actually *does* owing to its inherently dynamic, transitory nature. The experiential field, which of course includes attention, is constantly changing, continuously moving from one state to the next, wandering as it were from one point of focus to the next. Experience doesn't hold still. It's a shape-shifter…

Given this, could it be that the drifting of attentional focus is not the colossal problem it's been made out to be? I realize of course that what I am saying here flies in the face of conventional meditative wisdom. But as I said, the very drifting that meditators have struggled for millennia to overcome or keep in check is actually the natural state of things. "Drifting away" is, we could say, reality's signature mode! And so in placing ourselves in opposition to that natural tendency through any degree of mental effort, even if subtle, we may not only be fighting a losing battle but also reinforcing the notion that some portions of the experiential field are somehow preferable or more real than others.

With that consideration in mind, here's a very simple yet powerful practice you might enjoy experimenting with. You can listen to a recording of it at http://www.newharbinger.com/41818.

PRACTICE

As you sit here, just allow experience to do what it does. Notice the way in which attention naturally drifts from one point of focus to the next.

Feel the way in which experience moves and wafts and undulates, like the tides, shifting from moment to moment.

Now, as you notice this natural movement, if you suddenly find yourself having seemingly "lost contact" or "being less present" with this ceaseless drifting of experience, don't worry. That is just the next place the drifting has taken you!

Reality is just doing what reality does. Drifting...

This is life's nature, never to hold still. Like clouds moving through the vast and spacious sky, we are forever drifting, one state wafting into the next. Some focus of attention appears; some experiential moment comes into view. And then we suddenly find ourselves somewhere else, swept away yet again. But this drifting is not some spiritual mistake; it is simply what life does!

And so, there is no drifting away from reality for there is *only* reality, forever drifting into itself. Enjoy the drifting for there is really nothing else to enjoy!

The Problem of Oversimplification

As part of my work I teach graduate courses in research methods, so I certainly appreciate the value and validity of science as a method for inquiring into the nature of things. But so often, what we find in science, maybe by necessity, is a kind of gross overgeneralization. For example, the sciences with which I am most familiar tend to paint their explanatory pictures in very broad brushstrokes. Read any headline reporting on some finding in psychology or medicine and what you'll invariably find are fairly crude, oversimplified descriptions of the phenomena under study: "Eating this food helps prevent this disease; Certain early childhood experiences are correlated with particular behaviors later in life; Practicing meditation or taking these prescription medications can reduce the symptoms of depression; People who experience particular types of emotional reactions show this kind of brain activity"…and on and on it goes.

In all these examples, what the scientific findings are essentially saying, in one form or another, is that *on average*, if you do this, take this substance, or practice this therapeutic technique, this other thing will *tend* to happen. But of course, if you do therapy x or eat food y, you won't necessarily experience outcome z, because the explanatory models ("this causes that") are simply too overgeneralized, unsophisticated, and lacking in nuance. With or without the support of science, we might be inclined to say that on average, if you do this, that will happen. However, describing how things tend to behave, or how they correlate with other things, says nothing about how and what they specifically are, at least not in any definitive sense.

A great example of this type of imprecision is the phenomenon of personality inventories. The many typologies that are out there—the Myers-Briggs Type Indicator (The Myers & Briggs Foundation 2018) or the Enneagram (The Enneagram Institute 2017), to name but two—theoretically tell us something about the way people tend to behave, on average. Imagine for a moment a classic bell-shaped statistical curve that represents one's "personality"—the various qualities, characteristics, dispositions, and so on that make up who they are. The qualities a person displays most frequently would be illustrated by the midpoint and those areas that lie closer to the center of the bell curve. Then as you ventured out from either side of that central area, you would begin to encounter aspects of the person that diverge from his or her average or "usual" tendencies.

However, even if the person on average tends to more frequently display those qualities and characteristics that coalesce around the midpoint of the curve, the complete picture of who they are can only ever be captured by including the *entirety* of the curve—that is, the sum total of that person's qualities, not merely those they are the most likely to exhibit. So if, as we are prone to do, we categorize a person according to some personality typology or characterize them by some other psychological or biological classificatory system, we are by necessity oversimplifying who and what they are. I think this is one of the reasons I've found myself resistant to such typologies as I find them to be terribly unsatisfying in their generalizations, failing in the end to fully capture the infinitely rich, nuanced, multidimensional creatures that we are.

Whether we are scientists or not, it's interesting to consider this seemingly insatiable thirst to explain, reduce and, in the process, oversimplify reality. Of course it is understandable that we would search out the possible causes of our physical and psychological difficulties and in turn identify remedies to counter those apparent causal factors. The problem, however, lies in unquestioningly adopting any framework, whether it's based on science, philosophy, or religion. Interpretive frameworks represent incomplete and ultimately misleading renderings of reality, oversimplifications of a realm—human experience—that is exceedingly complex and ultimately irreducible.

As an example of this popular as well as scientific tendency, I recently came across an online article from *Forbes*, "The 7 Ways Meditation Can Actually Change the Brain" (Walton 2015). The author argues that the ancient benefits of these practices are now being confirmed by modern scientific methods such as EEG and FMRI. However, in point of fact, the relationship between meditative practices and brain activity is tenuous at best. The reality is that meditation practice is associated statistically with changes in different brain regions and networks but only in *some* people who practice and even in those people, only to some extent. It is so far from actually being a one-to-one correspondence ("do this practice and this change will happen in this particular way in your brain") that to talk about meditation being able to "change your brain" in specific and predictable ways is, well, laughable. Of course, this issue isn't unique to meditation—we find the same problem of oversimplifying cause/effect relationships with other therapeutic modalities as well, from psychotropic medications to psychotherapy.

Despite the amazing contributions neuroscience is making to our understanding of the human brain, the idea that we can take exceedingly complex phenomena such as thought and emotion and understand them solely in terms of, that is reduce them to, basic neuro-chemical activities and interactions is a prime example of the problem with oversimplification so rampant not just in science but everyday life.

Not surprisingly, language itself—the very medium through which the various forms of knowledge are transmitted—is also, by its very nature, reductionist. Regardless of the word—happiness, sorrow, joy, grief, cloud, mountain, pleasure, pain—language functions as a kind of conceptual shorthand, a way of collapsing exceedingly complex arrays of experiential phenomena into single descriptors. Language has considerable utility in so far as its capacity to convey a *general* impression of what is being seen, heard, felt, or touched in any given moment. But the experiences themselves can never be fully captured by the linguistic placeholders used to convey them. Phenomenal experiences we attempt to convey with such words as beautiful, delicious, painful, or infuriating can never actually be conveyed by those words because the experiences are far too vast, complex, and nuanced to be easily or accurately rendered by concepts and the language used to articulate them.

For example, take the state of mind we call anxiety. What is it? To be sure, we have a word and regularly employ that word to characterize a particular type of human experience. But what precisely is it that we're characterizing when we use the label "anxiety"? As we look up in the night sky and see that object called the "Big Dipper," we're essentially recognizing and then naming a particular patterning of light. Similarly, we could say that the phenomenon we label as "anxiety" refers to a distinctive pattern of experience, energy, and information. But naming that general pattern "anxiety" doesn't actually tell us very much about it as it leaves out the specific details, failing to capture the extraordinarily diverse and complex array of energies that constitute such an experience in its actuality.

We try to convey what's transpiring experientially by generalizing about those experiences, saying such things as "I went for a walk today and had a wonderful time," or "I had class tonight but it was really boring." And while such conceptual/linguistic renderings give us a very general impression about what took place and the nature of it, our experiences are made up of very specific details and *not* generalities, which are always abstractions *about* those specifics. When I say that I am "feeling anxious," I am sharing a generalized picture about what is being experienced and not its actuality, which cannot be reduced conceptually. Our definitions of things and experiences may represent a useful kind of communicational shorthand. But the actual experiences themselves are utterly beyond the concepts used to define them.

The bottom line is that human experiences and their putative causes transcend any and all explanatory models. The concepts we utilize to point to and describe the presence of specific experiences may be able to convey something about those phenomena but like the aforementioned personality inventories, the models will always fall short. In the final analysis, any modeling of reality will necessarily be an oversimplification.

Incidentally, this is as true in science as it is in spirituality. For just as neuroscience seems hell bent on reducing the complexity of human experience to electrochemical firings in the brain, so too do most spiritual teachings fall prey to their own brand of reductionism, taking the realm of human experience, which is by nature indescribable and multidimensional, and collapsing it into unidimensional concepts and descriptors such as spirit, light, God, or awareness that are themselves experientially inconceivable and irreducible.

In the final analysis, the territory we call experience is what's real; the scientific and spiritual maps, beautiful and elegant as they may be, are nothing more than mere abstractions, conceptual renderings of an actuality that cannot, in the end, be fairly rendered or conceived.

Signal and Noise

We tend to believe that reality is more or less coherent and structured. We imagine that there are observable objects (people, places, and things) and subjective states (thoughts, feelings, and sensations) that exist, and that can be clearly defined and conveyed via language.

However, the reality is that in every instant, we are being flooded by an inconceivable array of experiential phenomena. And while we tend not to recognize or appreciate it, the lion's share of what's being perceived doesn't actually fit together logically or cohere into any structured narrative or conceptual framework.

Because so much of what's happening experientially doesn't fit neatly into any of the narratives that we've come to believe, we try to maintain these apparently coherent ideas by essentially overlooking all the experiential data that doesn't fit those neat and tidy conceptual formulations.

In order to describe and seemingly make sense of things *as* things (that's a feeling, that's a thought, that's a human, that's a bird) we have to attend primarily to the "signal," those dimensions of experience that stand out as being coherent and describable, while censoring out and effectively treating as "noise" the vast array of uninterpretable or seemingly unrelated phenomena occurring every instant.

In a sense, we are signal snobs, believing those experiences that don't correspond to our structured narratives are essentially "noise in the system" that we can more or less disregard. However, by censoring out these less coherent, less structured elements of the experiential field that lie outside the bounds of ordinary human discourse and description, could it be that we are robbing ourselves of so much of life's inconceivable richness, dynamism, and vitality?

PRACTICE

As you sit here, just let yourself open to the full field of experience. Notice how much is actually present. Despite whatever interpretations may be operating, just appreciate how vast, how boundless, how endless the field of experience actually is.

How many different colors and subtle shades are being seen right now? You could never hope to count them all. How many different shapes are being perceived? And what about the astounding play of light and form?

Notice the way in which everything that's appearing in the visual field—the presence of light, shadow, reflection, shape, and color—is not merely being seen but also felt, even if subtly. Let yourself venture out to the very edges of the field of sight; what is felt there? You can't quite say and yet something still seems present.

Notice how everything that is being seen is here for only a flash instant.

And since there really is no permanence or constancy to any of it, how are we even able to create the sense that reality is somehow structured or coherent?

Look for yourself; is it actually possible to maintain a consistent plot-line when the experiential "story" keeps transforming into something else, moment by moment?

Notice the full field of whatever is being sensed and felt. You may have names for some of what's appearing. But look and see if you can notice those finer, subtler dimensions of experience for which there really is no language.

Feel the very subtle and oftentimes chaotic display of mental representations we call thinking? Can you sense how nonlinear and nonrational so much of that movement of mind is, the flashing, flickering, shimmering, ephemeral nature of it all?

Maybe what we think of as the predictable, seemingly boring and uninspiring structure and normalcy of our everyday lives is actually much more like a Jackson Pollock painting—mysterious, playful, colorful, exciting, carefree, dynamic, and unpredictable, impossible to understand or make sense of and yet astonishingly alive and exquisite in its incoherence and irrationality.

What Is Awareness?

Spiritual teachings frequently talk about awareness as a kind of special, privileged domain, one that is free of the comings and goings of phenomenal experience (see the chapter "The Knowing of This Moment Is the Feeling of It"). Awareness is often described as that which notices all the stories the mind generates and yet is neither defined by nor caught up in those mental interpretations.

However, when we speak of awareness in this way, as something that actually exists and is distinct from the arising and passing away of the phenomena it notices or observes, this presumes that awareness is a clearly identifiable, definable thing, distinct from other things. Let's investigate this assumption to see if it holds up...

PRACTICE

Right now, just notice the fact that you are awake and aware and see that this capacity to be aware is here without exerting a single ounce of effort to make it so.

Whatever is being experienced and however you may be defining it, you know that experience is present for one simple reason: because you are aware.

But here's the question: What exactly *is* awareness? Simply because we have a name for it doesn't mean we actually know what it is. So, what is it? What *is* awareness, not as an idea, but as an experience?

Whatever and wherever you feel that word awareness is pointing to, look right there, right in your own direct experience, and see if you can find what it is, what this word "awareness" is actually indicating experientially. What is awareness made of, texturally?

One way we might describe awareness is that it is composed of countless subtle experiential details which are themselves composed of more details which are in turn made of more details.

Can you feel that, the way in which this thing we call awareness is ultimately an inconceivable mystery, a mystery we can never get to the bottom of owing to its infinite subtlety and depth?

This inquiry can reveal that the very thing we imagined and presumed awareness to be is, in the final analysis, simply not knowable.

Awareness is, like every other experience, ultimately indefinable. Sure, we could say that awareness has a particular feel to it, a qualitative texture that is distinct from other dimensions of experience.

And yet, it's really impossible to characterize what exactly that is. In fact, the only real category in which we can safely place awareness is the "category" of indescribability, the transcendental, category-less common denominator of all experience.

Dialogue: *The Miracle of Everything*

Sara: In some of your talks and writings, I've heard you describe the nature of things as being "miraculous." But what exactly do you mean by this? It seems to me that while some things can't be explained scientifically and so could be called miraculous, to call everything in life a miracle seems, well, a stretch.

John: While conventionally we think of miracles as those things that defy explanation, the reality is that all phenomena defy explanation. If, for example, you saw a human being flying around without the aid of any mechanical device, you would say that's a miracle, right? On the other hand, people believe it's possible to explain, technically and scientifically, how a human being can travel above the earth with the aid of a helicopter or airplane.

Sara: Exactly. We can explain how people can fly in an airplane but not how they can fly on their own, without the aid of any flying machine.

John: It sure seems that way. But if we look a little deeper, it can be seen that we aren't *actually* explaining the things we imagine we're explaining, at least not comprehensively. The fact is that we don't understand the root origin or ultimate cause of *any* of the aerodynamic principles or engineering dynamics that allow for that seemingly explicable phenomenon we call flying in an airplane. Our explanations for the things we take for granted as normal and natural only go so far. We can explain how we're able to fly in airplanes…but only to a point.

Sara: I don't really understand. While I might not be able to explain it myself, a physicist or engineer could tell you exactly how planes are able to fly above the ground.

John: Fair enough. But let's look a little more closely at what we conventionally think of as the explicable or unmiraculous. In order to explain how we can fly in an airplane, we'd have to account for *every* aspect of that phenomenon, right? And yet we can't do this because the existence of one part of that equation, namely the one flying in the plane, can't be accounted for.

Sara: What do you mean that we can't account for the person flying
              the plane?

John: Well, what is it that allows for the existence of the organism we
              see operating the controls of the plane? How do we account for
              the fact of its consciousness, which is essential in order to fly
              the plane? The reality is that with or without the aid of any
              flying machine, no part of the existence of the person soaring
              above the earth can actually be explained, at least not
              definitively.

Sara: I'm still not sure I understand. Don't we understand how the
              body works, how the brain functions that enables us to do
              something like operate a machine?

John: Yes, and no. For example, for a mammal such as us to live, it
              must be able to breathe, right? But for breath to exist, there
              must be air. And in order for air to exist, there must be the
              right set of atmospheric conditions, which are themselves
              dependent on various other forces, such as gravity, that are in
              turn interacting with untold galactic and cosmic phenomena.

              In other words, we can't definitively explain even the most
              basic of human realities—breathing—without also explaining
              the unthinkably vast planetary and cosmic forces at play that
              enable such things as air and breath to be. And because they're
              inextricably linked to breathing, those universal forces would
              have to be explained in order to know in a precise and compre-
              hensive way what breathing actually was. And yet no such
              explanations exist.

              In other words, the actual existence of the breath is an
              absolute mystery and miracle, which means you and I and
              everyone are also miracles, whether we're flying in planes or
              soaring above the earth on our own.

              In the end, we're left with the reality that there is nothing
              but the miraculous, every aspect of this reality ultimately inex-
              plicable by its very nature and existence.

Wide Open

As humans we typically aspire to feel less closed and more open—more openhearted, open-minded, and so on. We seek to feel a greater sense of spaciousness in our lives, to feel less bounded, less shut down, less blocked or resistant, more receptive, unguarded, and undefended.

Given this aspiration, it is not surprising that psychological and spiritual traditions have developed an array of practices whose aim is to help people cultivate a greater sense of openness. However, as beneficial as such practices may be, they are typically rooted in a central and largely unquestioned assumption, namely that there is actually something that can be closed and subsequently opened up through some effort, cultivation, or practice. The following meditation invites us to consider a different possibility, that openness is always and already the nature of every moment, even those we conceive of and experience as more "closed down."

PRACTICE

As you sit here, simply notice how open everything is, how experience has no borders, no edges, no lines delineating or distinguishing one thing from the next.

Feel the swirl of sensations we call "body" and notice that they are pure openness.

See how you cannot locate the precise place where this dance of sensation begins or where it ceases to exist.

With eyes open, notice the field of vision, how wide open it is, how you cannot tell at what point the field of seeing comes to a definitive end.

Feel the endlessness of whatever is being seen, the complete openness of it.

And now simply feel your own aliveness, the energy, the felt sense of what you call "you." Feel the presence of your own being, your own existence.

Notice it too is wide open, without border or boundary. See how there are no clear edges to this life force and energy that you are. Notice how impossible it is to locate where this presence of aliveness begins or ends.

Appreciate this natural openness that you are and everything is, a seamlessness with nothing blocking or in the way of anything else.

No Hierarchy

In each instant, we are being barraged by a flood of experiential phenomena. Based in large part on the ways in which we conventionally define and categorize the many things we encounter in life, our tendency is to divide reality up into those experiences we like, those we don't much care for, and those we're kind of neutral about. But, for these next few moments, I invite you to experiment with another possibility, that the experiential hierarchies we've created and tended to believe in as givens are based on the ways in which we conventionally characterize phenomena which, as we've been exploring throughout the book, are in their essence undefinable. You can download a recording of the following practice at http://www.newharbinger.com/41818.

PRACTICE

For these next few moments, I invite you to explore what it might be like to play no favorites, to experiment with letting go of any hierarchy whatsoever, relaxing the habit of privileging or elevating some experiential moments over others.

But remember, no hierarchy means just that. So, if you should find yourself evaluating, judging, or thinking that some things hold greater value or importance than others, then that's fine too! In other words, rather than seeing judging or evaluating as being somehow inferior to a state of non-judging or non-evaluating, simply allow *everything* to be equal.

Let yourself entertain the possibility that no experience, no disposition, no mode is intrinsically higher, better, or more meaningful than any other.

See what it's like to come to your experience in this way, opening yourself up to the possibility that everything you encounter, everything that's experienced is equal in its relevance, equal in its importance, equal in its value and equal in its beauty, all of it an inconceivable miracle, simply because it is.

Time

Time represents one of the most taken-for-granted dimensions of the human experience. As part of what we might call conventional reality, the existence of time is more or less a given. It seems irrefutable that time exists. Of course, we have plenty of evidence to support this conventional view that time is real. It certainly seems to comport with our lived experience. But does it? Do we *actually* experience something called "time?" Or, is it possible that the notion of time and its passage depends upon a kind of abstraction, a conceptual interpretation for which there isn't in fact any supporting experiential evidence?

It certainly seems that we have evidence of a past that has been and a future that has yet to become. However, to create the impression of time, we must literally imagine past and future into existence via the mechanism of memory and thought. But experientially, we have never encountered anything resembling a past or future. All we have ever actually experienced is this flash instant, this ever-changing, ever-fluctuating *now*.

The following meditation explores this question of time and its reality, or lack thereof. You can download a recording of it at http://www.newharbinger.com/41818.

PRACTICE

Beginning with this thing we call "the past," can you locate something, some experience that was? Where is the direct experiential evidence of that which you call "past?"

Sure, we can imagine an apparent past via the miracle of memory. But as an actuality, it doesn't exist.

Try to put yourself there. It's not possible, for the imagined past only ever exists now, in this very instant, this moment of aliveness.

What we call the past is an abstraction, an idea. It exists as a thought, a thought that is only ever appearing *now*. There is no *then*. We may peer into what we refer to as the past but that looking is always occurring right now, in the immediacy of *what is*.

Just as the past cannot be found, neither can what we call the future. To be sure, we can imagine what will be. But we can never actually arrive there. We are never able to experience anything resembling a future. All

our envisioning of some impending moment only ever occurs in the immediacy of now. What we call *the future* is sheer fantasy. It does not exist as
an actuality.

There is only ever this flash instant in which the thought of what
might be can arise. As with what was, what might be is not an actuality for
there is only what is.

Now let's explore this notion of *what is*, the so-called now.

Look at your direct experience and see if something called the present
moment can actually be found. Look at what's appearing—something is
clearly here. But this here is in a constant state of flux, right? What we call
the present appears and then is gone in a flash.

Look and see how experience doesn't freeze or hold still. Whatever
instantaneous perception we might locate and say, "Here it is, here is the
present moment. I've found the now," that now has already disappeared
and become something else before we can even name or describe it. Notice
the way in which reality is in constant motion, never holding still, forever
slipping away as soon as it appears.

There really is no such thing as a discernible moment that is bounded,
a "now" that has an identifiable beginning, middle, or end.

And so, in reality, no past, present, or future can ever be found to
exist.

Notice that in experience, there is no time for the very instant the
moment springs forth, it transforms itself, always being and yet forever
becoming something else. Feel this timelessness, the unstoppable, ever-
changing flow we call reality.

The Freedom of Uncertainty

Many traditions hold the belief that to be free of the grip of conceptual thinking and the grasping, identification, and suffering it purportedly gives rise to, we must either quiet the mind's activity or discover a part of us that is already conceptually quiet and beyond the reach of thought. In such teachings, one is frequently directed to notice and rest as *the awareness that knows or is awake to the movement of the mind* but is neither caught in nor defined by such activity (see the chapter "What Is Awareness?"). However, as true as it may be that awareness is beyond thought, it turns out that *all* experiences, including thinking itself, are by nature beyond the reach of conceptualization and are ultimately indefinable. And because of this, there is no reason to privilege one aspect of reality (awareness) over another (thought) since both are equal in terms of their being unfathomable, indescribable expressions of life. Here's an experiment... You can download a recording of it at http://www.newharbinger.com/41818.

PRACTICE

For a moment, think some thought, maybe the idea of what you will be doing for dinner later tonight.

Once you have that thought in mind, just feel the presence of it—something is undoubtedly there and you know that it is there, right? Something is showing up experientially which we label as "thinking." But what exactly does that word tell us about the specifics of what is being experienced?

What is thought, actually?

What is thinking made of, experientially?

We use this term "thought" to describe a particular domain of experience. But while it may be indicative of something we encounter, otherwise we wouldn't have evolved such a word in the first place, whatever thinking actually is cannot be neatly collapsed into any conceptual or linguistic category. The word "thought" may convey some vague, general sense of the actual territory it is endeavoring to describe. But that is all words and concepts can ever do.

Language is simply not capable of capturing with any sort of completeness or precision the intricately rich subtlety and nuance that constitutes every instant including the experience we call thinking. However helpful they may be as pointers, the words we use to categorize and order the world of experience don't actually tell us very much about the specific details of anything.

To further illustrate this point, let's examine another phenomenon, color. As you gaze into a clear sky, you know there is a word—blue—to describe what you're seeing. But just as with the word "thought," the conceptual label "blue," while indicative of something, conveys very little about what we *actually* experience when we see something blue.

The experience of blueness cannot be characterized—it's so infinitely subtle and deep. And just as with thought, we can ask the same question of the experience of blue—what is it? What does blue *feel* like? What is this thing called blue actually made of experientially?

The exploration of these questions reveals that they are not ultimately answerable because we can never quite get to the bottom of what anything is.

Simply feel the presence of any phenomenon and you will begin to notice this—that despite the immense vocabularies we've developed to characterize the countless and diverse forms life can take, each and every experience is utterly beyond any way we might imagine or conceive it to be. It's quite extraordinary, isn't it, the ultimate indefinability of everything?

Can you sense the freedom of this, the freedom of not being certain about what anything is?

Dialogue: *The World Is Made of Verbs*

Maria: I've heard you say that we can't actually know what things are. What do you mean by this? It seems I have all sorts of knowledge of what things are or aren't...

John: Well, if we want to know what a thing is, we must have some point of reference to compare it to. But if things are as impermanent as they appear to be and by virtue of that relentless dynamism, utterly unique, never repeating, then there's no way to definitively know what anything is. In other words, if I've never seen or experienced this present phenomenon before, I can't possibly know what it is.

From this vantage, knowledge is essentially a pretense, an oversimplified, overgeneralized association the mind makes between what's presently being experienced and something we imagine, through memory, has occurred before.

Maria: I don't know. It seems we have to act as though things and events have a kind of permanence. And for most practical purposes many physical things do, like the dollar bill in my wallet. Even periodic events like a sunrise or an ocean tide can be treated as more or less the same as the previous one, even though we may realize that each new one is in certain respects unique. If it were any other way, there'd be no continuity to life, no flow, no time.

John: Maybe there *is* no actual continuity or time.

Maria: What do you mean?

John: To be sure, it *seems* as if time and continuity are actualities. But the provocative question I'm posing here is, do they in fact exist as we imagine they do?

We may not like the implications of what we discover when we look beyond our presuppositions of what things are. However, things rarely conform to the way we imagine or believe them to be. We may not like confronting the possibility that what we think is true may *not* be the case. But whether it's the conventional notion that things have permanence, continuity, or anything else, the question I'm interested in is, "Is what we believe to be true *actually* true?"

I'm not suggesting there's anything wrong with acting as though things have some degree of permanence. Clearly we do this and it would appear to have some pragmatic utility, maybe even necessity. At the same time, the reality I'm pointing to—that what we're seeing now is *not* in fact the same as what we were seeing a moment ago because of the inherently unstable, dynamic nature of everything—*also* has immense practical utility.

Maria: How so?

John: Well, for one, recognizing the uniqueness of each instant—the newness, the freshness of everything—facilitates many of the things we aspire to experience more in life, such as greater appreciation, gratitude, and awe. Jesus purportedly said, "unless ye become like little children, ye cannot enter the kingdom…" (Matthew 18:3). I think what he meant was that the child is not yet burdened by knowledge of what the world is. For the very young, *everything* is a wonder, an awe-inspiring miracle, because it has quite literally never before been seen. The newly born have yet to accumulate knowledge of what things are. Because of this, they see with that profound openness and innocence that we adults find so compelling and beautiful.

What the Zen Buddhists call "beginner's mind" is natural to the child. And while it may be more difficult to reach once we've developed the knowledge of what things appear to be, it's still quite possible to recognize the inherently unique nature of every instant of perception. We have quite literally never seen this instant before, nor will we ever see it again. And that's a powerful thing to realize.

Here's another practical application of what I'm pointing to…

Human beings, as a rule, struggle with letting go of things—the past, judgments, beliefs, grudges, stories, and so on. And while we may experience letting go to be difficult, maybe even impossible, we believe this as a result of one inno-cent misperception, that experiences endure and have stability.

However, if we look a bit more closely, we can discover that letting go is the easiest, most effortless thing because it's the very nature of reality. Life is quite literally letting go of itself each instant owing to its inherently unstable, transient nature. We may speak conventionally about striving or struggling to let go of this, that, or the other thing. But the truth is that holding on is what's impossible, not letting go.

Life has *already* taken the past away because that's what life does. It dissolves what was, gives rise to what is, and then dissolves that too, no sooner than it appears. This is the unrelenting, ever-changing nature of experience. And so we don't need to work or practice accepting and letting go of things, since whatever occurred has *already* been let go of, already been forgiven, already been allowed. As the Tibetans say, experiences "self-liberate upon arising."

Finally, through recognizing the discontinuous, impermanent nature of phenomena, we discover that nothing is static, nothing remains the same. This discovery reveals that the things we imagine we're bound by, caught up in, or troubled by don't actually exist, at least not as the discrete, concrete things we've imagined them to be. For something to exist as a "thing" that we could be stuck in, there would have to be persistence, which direct investigation shows is not in fact the case.

Since there is no endurance to phenomena owing to the ever-changing nature of things, the world is, in a very real sense, made of verbs, not nouns.

The Bottomless Well of Infinity

It seems reasonable to imagine that the closer we look at some object, whether it's seemingly external or internal to us, the more capable we will be of discerning what that object actually is. We think, not surprisingly, that by carefully examining a phenomenon, its disparate parts will somehow converge, moving toward greater and greater clarity, coherence, and definability, revealing the essence of whatever is being observed. We believe that if we look close enough, eventually we'll come to know what makes a star a star, a cloud a cloud, a molecule a molecule, or a person a person.

However, it doesn't actually work that way; it turns out that the more carefully we examine things, the less coherent they become. Instead of discovering greater resolution and specificity ("Oh, *that's* what that is"), what we find the closer we look is more and more information, detail, and diversity. Paradoxically, the deeper we delve into the nature of things, the *less* clear we become about what they actually are!

PRACTICE

Imagine your exploration of some phenomenon to be like traveling down a deep well. You think that when you get to the end of your investigations, you'll find yourself standing on firm ground at the bottom of the well, having finally come to a clear understanding of what that particular phenomenon actually is. And yet it doesn't work that way.

Take, for example, a tree. From one vantage, we see this familiar visual object and recognize it as belonging to the category of things we call "trees." But as we travel down our metaphorical well and draw closer to it, investigating what the tree is composed of, we discover it is made up of countless details such as leaves, branches, bark, and color. If we then proceed farther down the well, examining those details we've identified, we'll find those parts of the tree are themselves composed of more details (cells, molecules, atoms, electrons). And if we look further into those details, we'll find even more of the same, ad infinitum.

While it may seem to defy common logic, the reality is that the closer we look at objects or experiences, the less clear it is what exactly we're looking at. Choose anything that might be showing up right now in your field of experience. It doesn't matter what it is. For example, pick some emotional state you're experiencing. Maybe you're feeling a little restless or agitated. Or maybe you're experiencing a sense of calm or ease. In either case (agitation or calm), just feel whatever is present. Now, get very, very close to it. Whether you call it agitation or calm, just look as carefully as you can at whatever is happening. And now, move in even closer. What exactly *is* this state? Agitation, calm…these labels are pointing to something. The question is, what exactly *is* that? What are those words actually referring to?

As you continue to look very, very closely, exploring this question, you might find yourself answering that the mental-emotional state being experienced is composed of various sensations. Okay. Now get right up as close as you can to what you're calling "sensations," and ask the same question: What are *those* made of? As you continue in this way, traveling down the metaphorical well of your experience, you may begin to notice something quite remarkable: that the closer you look, the more intimate you become with whatever is happening experientially, the less clear it is exactly what you're looking at! It's a strange and curious thing, isn't it, that as we draw closer to things, investigating what experiences are actually made of, those experiences seem to move away from us, like a receding horizon that we can never quite reach, no matter how many steps we might take toward it.

And so, to return to our metaphorical well, the more we investigate the nature of things, the clearer it becomes that we cannot know definitively what any object or experience actually is because everything is beyond the reach of our definitions and categories. While at first glance, this may seem disorienting or frustrating, it turns out to be a powerful and liberating discovery for it reveals that all our imagining that we are bound up in, defined by, or limited by experiences is just that—pure imagination, because there is no bottom to the well. We are forever falling through the indescribability that is everything.

The Borderless Field of Being

By and large, the consensus human view is that we exist as separate individuals, bio-psycho-social-spiritual organisms encased in these physical bodies that are clearly distinguishable from the outer environments in which they appear to reside. Put another way, our tendency is to perceive ourselves as separate subjects navigating a world of objects. We believe that these bounded creatures we see ourselves as are somehow cut off and effectively separate from the rest of existence. But maybe it only *appears* that way (see the chapter "Boundaries").

Let's explore our own existence and see if we can find a clear point where what we think of as "ourselves" ends and the world "outside" of us begins... You can download a recording of this practice at http://www. newharbinger.com/41818.

PRACTICE

Notice that you are here, that you are alive. Let yourself feel this simple fact, the undeniable presence of your own existence, the simple feeling of being.

Notice that no effort is required for this to be so—no strategies, no techniques, no manipulations are needed to create this sense of aliveness; it is naturally present, existence streaming forth spontaneously, generating and sustaining itself, moment by moment.

As you feel the presence of this field of being, let yourself venture out to the farthest edges of it—can you find anything there, any point where the field of being comes to an end? Can you locate a line separating the field from anything else? Or is there just an edgeless continuum of being, without border or boundary?

Notice that no matter what might be occurring within this boundaryless field, being remains as it is, unalterably alive and present.

Feel the way in which the field is not circumstance dependent—a thousand different thoughts, feelings, and sensations can appear and disappear and all the while the field remains. Being continues to be, existence continues to exist, no matter the shape or form it may take.

Feel the ease, the fullness, the rich lusciousness of being.

While we may imagine ourselves to be these isolated creatures, vulnerable subjects in a world of objects and circumstances, see that, experientially, this is not the case.

Feel the way in which the field of being, the field of experience itself is actually seamless, an indivisible, all-inclusive expanse, an edgeless space of invulnerability that nothing can harm for there is nothing apart from it.

Here you are, sitting here. And yet there is no finality to you, no point where beingness ceases to be, no place where the edge of "you" comes to an end. Feel this.

Revel in the vast, luscious infinity that you are.

No Distractions

In most meditative traditions, the practitioner is encouraged to maintain focus on some object or aspect of experience and then, whenever they find their mind wandering off and becoming distracted by something else, bring attention back to that focus.

While this kind of concentrative, focused attention can no doubt be experienced as beneficial, it can also contribute to its fair share of frustration and tension, given the mind's propensity to become captivated by all sorts of phenomena. Along with the experience of frustration that can often occur when we make an effort to control or regulate the flow of attention, such approaches can also end up reinforcing the idea that the mind's tendency to move from one thing to another is necessarily a problem that must be rectified.

Approaches that emphasize attentional control can also lead us to conclude that some states (such as being focused) are somehow preferable to others (being distracted), effectively blinding us to the mystery and miracle that underlies *all* experiences, regardless of how we might conventionally label them.

Finally, since attention, like every other phenomenon, is never the same from moment to moment owing to its inherently dynamic, impermanent nature, the effort to keep it still and unmoving may turn out to be a literal impossibility. You can listen to a recording of the following practice at http://www.newharbinger.com/41818.

PRACTICE

For these next few moments, I invite you to experiment with letting go completely of any effort to control attention. Allow the mind to go wherever it wishes to go. Notice that even if you try to keep attention fixed somewhere, or stay focused on some aspect of experience, the mind doesn't remain anywhere for very long.

Given this tendency of mind, wherever attention may happen to alight, simply let it be there, allowing it to linger however long it wishes. If the mind naturally focuses on something, then let that focus be as it is.

And if attention feels completely dispersed and unfocused, jumping from here to there, darting from one thing to the next, like a butterfly flitting about, then simply allow that to be as well.

Let it be perfectly okay that the mind does whatever it does, goes wherever it goes, moves however it moves.

Enjoy the pleasure, the ease, and the freedom as you let go of trying to direct or control attention and simply allow the mind to be as it is.

Consider the possibility that there are no distractions. See that what we might typically conceive of as a meditative distraction—for example, thinking or daydreaming—is simply another moment, another phenomenon arising in the field of experience.

To say that some experiences are distractions while others are not is really to privilege certain moments over others.

So instead of viewing particular experiences as distractions that we must keep ourselves from being distracted by, simply see that everything we might label as a distraction is in fact a miraculous apparition, an astounding occurrence of reality. See that there are no distractions but only different flavors, different modes, different textures of experience.

For these next moments, simply let there be no distractions but only experiences.

The Olympic Athlete Model of Spirituality

Humans are not born virtuoso musicians or world-class athletes. No, they must develop such capacities and mastery. But in the case of realizing the indivisible, inseparable nature of things that many spiritual traditions speak of, the Olympic athlete-virtuoso model, which one frequently finds championed in many of these same traditions, really doesn't apply.

Why? Because inseparability isn't actually a skill one must develop, like playing an instrument or excelling in a sport. It is simply the way reality is. One is not born being able to play the piano like Oscar Peterson or shoot a basketball like Michael Jordan. No, one must practice for many hours a day for many, many years to realize such virtuosity.

But when it comes to recognizing the singular nature of reality, no skill is required. Instead, anyone can simply look and see that right now, with no practice required, indivisibility is already given, already the case, already fully, one hundred percent the way life is, the way *you* already are.

PRACTICE

For a moment, look for yourself and see if you can find a seam in the universe of your experience, a clear line demarcating this from that, a boundary separating one thing from another, dividing this moment from the next.

Are there any such lines to be found? Is reality actually made of separate pieces? Or is there only this vast, undivided field of experiencing, utterly seamless by its very nature? Look and it can be plainly seen that all there is, is inseparability.

And so, since it is already the nature of every moment and experience, realizing that reality is undivided *must* be the easiest thing in the world, right? See right now that nothing need be done to make reality what it is—seamlessly whole, free of even one iota of separation or division.

If one wants to argue that it takes practice to realize this, then let the practice be to simply see that this is already the case, to look and see that undivided is simply the nature of things, the way reality has always been.

Dialogue: *The Many Flavors of Here*

John: While spiritual traditions are fond of telling us that we must strive to be more present, more aware, more "here," the reality is that *here is all there is.*

Raj: What do you mean, exactly?

John: Well, the one thing we can be certain of is that something is happening, right? Call it life, call it experience. It doesn't really matter. The point is that something is always here. From this vantage, there can be no entering or exiting here, no finding or losing it. Here is self-sustaining and self-generating, with each fleeting moment transforming itself into the next.

Raj: But what's appearing, this "here" as you call it, is always changing, right?

John: To be sure, each flash of experience carries its own distinctive flavor. Sweet is not sour; light is not sound; thought is not feeling; blue is not red. But regardless of the particular flavor on display, it's all simply here. Look at anything and ask yourself, "Where am I seeing this?" Listen to any sound. Where is it occurring? Feel any feeling or think any thought and notice where those are arising. Whether we imagine events to be occurring inside or outside the body's skin line, experience is always experienced, right *here.*

Raj: But isn't there something "over there," something that's apart from us, something that's not here?

John: Well, even if we say something is happening "over there," that experience still happens *here.* In experiencing, there are essentially zero degrees of separation between the subject or experiencer and the object which is being experienced. Nothing could be more intimate than experience. It's closer than close. Nearer than near...

Raj: What exactly do you mean when you say "closer than close"?

John: For a moment, just feel into the presence of this "here" in which experience is showing up spontaneously and continuously. As you explore the space of here, notice how it has no identifiable borders or edges to it, no boundary, no center, no circumference. We cannot, for example, tell where here ends and not-here, or "there," begins.

The reality of experience is that it's simultaneously here but also not here, present yet not able to be found as any clearly identifiable, discrete thing. This is the paradox of "here": it's not findable and yet it's undeniably present, exploding with infinite and unfathomable dimensionality, aliveness, depth, and meaning.

Raj: I'm not sure I understand what you're saying. It strikes me as kind of abstract.

John: I can appreciate that the way I'm speaking about this may seem a little abstract or overly philosophical, but it's really not. What it is, is paradoxical.

Raj: What do you mean by paradoxical?

John: Every experience presents as distinctive; a rose is not the sun is not the sea. But when we explore exactly what it is that constitutes each of these unique experiential flavors, we discover something quite remarkable—we can't seem to locate or identify exactly what is there.

Look for yourself at any experience. Let's say it's the feeling of being cold or warm. Something is clearly present; the words are pointing to something. The conceptual labels seem to refer to some specific pattern of experiential phenomena. And yet paradoxically when we find or locate those specifics, we come up empty-handed. It can't be said exactly what cold or warm is.

So, when I say that experiences are here but not here, present yet unfindable, this is what I mean.

Just as you might feel the wind or the splash of cold water upon your face, simply *feel* the vitality and power of whatever is here, this blazing aliveness that is present as each experiential apparition, each spontaneous, unpredictable eruption of life.

See the blue of the sky, the red of the rose? *Here.*

Feel the cold of the rain or the warmth of the sun? *Here.*

Listen to the roar of the sea, the deafening sounds of the city, or the quiet of the night? *Here.*

Each experience that appears is simply the unique taste of reality in that instant, the many flavors of here.

Everything's a One-Off

When we encounter some mental-emotional state such as fear or happiness, or some perceptual object such as a tree or a house, such phenomena are recognized as familiar owing to their particular patterning or the elements they appear to be composed of. It is through this mechanism of comparing and contrasting the moment that is presently arising with previous moments we imagine we've encountered before that we are able to place experiences in some familiar category of knowledge.

However, as real as it may seem to us that we know what things and experiences are and what descriptive categories or classification schemes they belong to, this entire process rests upon a kind of hallucination that overlooks the ways in which each momentary perception is utterly unique, never before seen. This particular feeling, thought, person, place, or thing may *seem* familiar to us. But is it actually the same or does it only appear that way owing to the power of this unreliable though miraculous thing we call memory? Let's have a look.

PRACTICE

Notice that the present moment is here for a flash, and then gone. Appreciate that you cannot locate what you imagine was appearing a moment ago, other than as a memory.

And even if you imagine that what's appearing this instant has been seen, felt, or experienced before, the reality is that it has not. This moment is utterly unique; it has never, ever happened. And it will never appear again, at least not like this.

It is true that events can often occur that we associate, through memory, with similar prior events. However, there will *always* be differences, not only in the events themselves but also in the larger context within which they are arising.

Notice that because this momentary experience has never been here before, at least not like this, you cannot actually know what it is. See that there is no category of knowledge to fairly place things in because any category could only ever be based on what we imagine was previously experienced.

To be sure, we engage in this conventional defining and categorizing, but only because we're not looking closely enough. We're assuming that what's appearing experientially fits some category of prior experience when the truth is that it cannot, for it has never been registered before.

You see, everything is a one-off and hence ultimately unknowable, at least as far as referencing it to some other moment we imagine has come before.

Awareness Is Experience

Many teachings emphasize the distinction between awareness and its content, instructing the practitioner to turn his or her attention away from the ever-changing flow of thoughts, feelings, and sensations and notice that which *knows* or is *aware* of all this coming and going (see the chapter "What Is Awareness?"). This can be a powerful practice for through it, one can discover awareness as a kind of stable, ever-present, clear, and spacious ground that is, in a sense, not affected by whatever content may be occurring within it.

In this modeling of reality, awareness (that which knows) is frequently portrayed as a special, separate, privileged domain apart from, untouched by, and free of its perceived content (that which is being known). However, let's look to see if this purported separation between awareness and its experiential content can actually be found.

PRACTICE

As you sit here, simply notice whatever is happening. Thoughts, feelings, sensations, sounds, sights, colors, textures—it matters not what specific objects are appearing; just let yourself notice whatever is present.

Now let your attention or awareness shift its focus from the objects being perceived to the fact of perceiving itself. Allow awareness to become aware of itself, to appreciate its own existence.

While framing things in this way, distinguishing awareness from its content, can bring about various benefits, let's explore whether this apparent distinction can actually be found.

Experience is happening, right? That seems undeniable. But how do you know experience is here? Well, however the experience may be described, you know it is present because there is awareness of it, otherwise you wouldn't know that anything was happening. Put another way, without awareness, there would be no experiences to report!

Now some teachings claim that there exists a domain of so-called "pure" awareness that is somehow completely free or devoid of experience, an awareness that has no phenomenal content present in it. But just as experience depends upon awareness for its existence, could it be that awareness depends upon the presence of experience for *it* to be? Let's investigate this question.

If I ask, "Are you aware?" and you answer "Yes," how is it that you are able to know this? How do you know you are aware? You know that awareness is present because you are experiencing it. In other words, without the experience of awareness, it effectively doesn't exist! No experience, no awareness. And no awareness, no experience!

You see, awareness and the experiences it reveals co-arise. They are really a single movement; you never find one without the other.

Look right now and notice this. See that you cannot tell where the awareness that illuminates this moment ends and the moment itself begins. A thought arises. But the arising of that thought is really inseparable from the awareness that reveals it, right?

You could never know a thought existed without awareness present to notice its existence. So in a very real sense, the arising of some experience is at the same time the arising of awareness.

The appearance of some momentary thought, feeling, or sensation is at the same time the appearance of awareness. The emergence of any experience is the emergence of awareness. They are inseparable. It's like a coin. On one side is the description of whatever is presenting itself—a happy thought, a sad feeling, a blissful or painful sensation...And on the other side of the coin is the awareness that reveals that particular experiential texture or quality.

But it's always a single coin. Indivisible. The knowing and the known, the subject and the object, the perceiver and the perceived, seemingly distinguishable as two things and yet ultimately an indistinguishable whole.

This that is present—should we call it experience or awareness? Well, maybe it's both. Or maybe we can't really say what it ultimately is! It's simply This. This indescribability...

So, just notice right now that as you are experiencing whatever you're experiencing, you are at the same time experiencing awareness.

And because experiencing never comes to a stop, what we might call "recognizing awareness" must also by definition be uninterrupted. In other words, contrary to how it is often framed, there's really no need to try to sustain awareness, for awareness is self-sustaining as the flow of experiencing itself.

There is no actual place to go to "find" something called "awareness." There's no need to quiet or stop thinking to be able to recognize awareness. Awareness is simply this—*this* perception, *this* thought, *this* feeling, *this* sensation, *this* present experience. After all, what else could awareness possibly be but this that is being experienced?

The Fullness of Experience

As a rule, we humans seem to be in a state of near perpetual seeking, driven and at times plagued by this sense that we are somehow lacking. And so we attempt to overcome this feeling of lack, this nagging sense that *something* is missing by filling ourselves with whatever experiences, relationships, entertainment, recognition, or possessions we imagine will fill the apparent void.

Now while this relentless searching after things is frequently portrayed as *the* spiritual bogeyman, there's really nothing wrong with it. It's just one of the things we tend to do as humans. It's completely innocent and, we could say, totally natural to seek to bring into our lives whatever it is we feel inspired to taste more of...

But even as we continue in this way, seeking whatever circumstances or experiences we are inclined to realize more of in our lives, we can at the same time notice something quite remarkable: This moment is *already* completely full.

"What do you mean?" you might ask. "I definitely feel that my life is missing not just some things, but *many* things. I definitely feel a sense of lack in my life, so how can you say that this moment is already full?"

It's a fair question, to be sure. But here is what I would invite you to consider: regardless of how you might label it, your experience is always full of whatever it is you're experiencing. Feel a sense of what you might call lack or emptiness? Then that is what you are full of! Experiencing great joy? Then *that* is what you are full of. Feel a tremendous sense of sorrow or grief? Just feel how full that is, full of that particular experience.

Here's a short practice to explore this.

PRACTICE

Imagine your experience like a room without walls. The room may be full of many different things—it could be full of something we might label as sorrow or joy. It may be full of what we would call clarity or confusion, lack or fulfillment.

But no matter how the content or condition of this moment might be described, the room of experience is always full, always complete.

"Full of what?" you might ask.

Full of experience itself...

See, there are no holes, no empty spaces, no sections of the room that are somehow lacking in experience. There is only ever the presence of experiencing filled with nothing but itself, as far as the eye can see. Just let yourself feel how full this vast, borderless, wall-less room of experiencing is—full of the presence, the vitality, the aliveness of whatever is here.

The Surface Is the Deep

In many teachings, we often hear things framed in terms of there being a surface or gross level of existence which is then contrasted with some supposedly deeper, truer, subtler layer or dimension of reality. But actually the deepest, subtlest depths are not found behind, below, or beneath but smack dab in the middle of the so-called gross or surface level of things.

Infinity doesn't lie in some realm beyond the apparently bounded or finite world. No, right here in the simplest, most ordinary of sensations and perceptions lies the most profound depth and boundlessness. All that's needed to realize this is to begin to appreciate that every experience, whether we label it as gross or subtle, superficial or deep, is by its very nature infinite and transcendental in so far as being beyond any possibility of categorization or description.

PRACTICE

Notice that within every sensation and perception, there is an inconceivable depth.

The taste of sugar on the tongue, the feel of wind on your cheek, the ocean's roar, the reflection of sunlight dancing on the morning dew—these everyday experiences are, each in their own way, completely beyond comprehension.

Simply feel the presence of your experience right now; can you sense the ways in which it contains an infinite number of dimensions and textures?

The transcendent nature of reality is not veiled, hidden behind some grosser, more surface-level way of perceiving things. No, the most profound, unfathomable depths are one hundred percent present in and as every single perception. And so right now, there is no need to venture to some other place or time to find greater depth because it is already here, present as the total indescribability of even the most ordinary human perceptions and experiences.

See that robin in the tree? There is no more profound truth, no greater spiritual dimension to be found, no hidden depth lurking in some other realm or plane of existence beyond whatever seemingly mundane, commonplace experiences we may be having.

No, the deepest, farthest reaches of reality are present right here and now in the most ordinary and obvious of perceptions, universes upon universes contained in even the simple act of seeing a red-breasted bird sitting perched on a tree.

So you see, there's no need to struggle to get beneath or beyond the surface of things to realize some greater depth, because the supposed "surfaces" of life are, themselves, immeasurably deep.

Overdramatizing the Path

I used to imagine that I knew what things were in some sort of definitive sense. I had certain maps I invoked to make sense of and describe reality, ways of framing either the spiritual path I was on or the one I was inviting others to take up. And while I didn't see it then, I now realize that I had overly dramatized the spiritual journey and its purported goals (such as enlightenment, realization, and awakening). In spiritual circles, it has become near gospel that the process of human transformation is going to be an exceedingly difficult, painful, disorienting, concept-destroying one, an arduous path in which we literally have to die to and surrender everything we've ever believed to be true about ourselves or life.

It sounds so dramatic, doesn't it, to give up *everything* for the sake of truth—all our desires, all our beliefs, all our control? The question is, is it really true? Must we give up everything or let go in such an absolute, dramatic way to achieve profound transformation? What if all of this dramatizing and romanticizing of the spiritual path wasn't necessary? What if we didn't need to surrender anything? What if it wasn't required (or even possible) to give up all beliefs, to stop thinking or interpreting and surrender the so-called ego?

Could it be that it's possible, and maybe even more effective, to engage in spiritual practice and inquiry without this dramatic sense of urgency and seriousness? What if we could come to it more in the spirit of light-hearted curiosity and playfulness? Could it be that the overly romanticized, do-or-die, "I must surrender and die to the separate self at all costs" mentality is precisely what perpetuates the sense that we are, in fact, bound, stuck, separate selves in the first place?

What I've observed is that this tendency to dramatize and absolutize what must happen for people to wake up and remain awake spiritually has the unintended consequence of perpetuating the fundamental illusion, the idea that we were ever actually asleep or separated from reality (or God if you prefer) in the first place. Telling seekers that they must "give up the false self" or "rest unceasingly in awareness" ends up perpetuating as much if not more misunderstanding than it clears up. Believing we must surrender thoughts, beliefs, or the self-sense serves to reify or concretize those very things. Proclaiming that the spiritual aspirant must give up control, drop the separate self, or abide in awareness serves to perpetuate the illusion that such experiences are actually obstacles to reality rather than expressions of it.

What if we could have our proverbial cake and eat it too? What if we could experience a sense of being an individual and continue having beliefs, desires, and so on and at the same time, recognize that all these characterizations of human experience are themselves utterly beyond the ways in which we tend to characterize or define them? What if it wasn't so much letting go of all that we believe in, giving up control, or surrendering ourselves but instead, simply seeing that these supposed "things"—control/letting go of control, surrendering/failing to surrender, recognizing awareness/failing to recognize awareness—are, themselves, *all* already infinite and wholly transcendental in their very nature and existence, transcendent in the sense of being beyond characterization?

The conventional spiritual narrative is that we are confused human beings trapped in some nightmarish illusion that we must, like heroic figures in some grand drama, awaken and extricate ourselves from once and for all. However, what if this simply weren't true? What if rather than having to liberate ourselves from bondage, confusion, or lack of awareness, we simply needed to see, if we're so inclined, that those experiences are not what we've imagined them to be based on the limited and partial ways we've tended to define them? What if we needn't give up control or the self but, instead, merely see—in a playful, curious way and whenever we feel moved to—that the experiences we label as "needing to be in control," "feeling we're in bondage," or "losing contact with awareness" are themselves expressions of a boundless, fathomless, inconceivable reality?

Could it be that no experience need be let go of or transcended, because every moment of experiencing is *already* transcendental, already infinite owing to its indefinable, indeterminate nature?

Identity and the Body of Experience

The list of things we can identify with in any given moment is a long one—body, mind, religion/spirituality, politics, sports teams, our personalities, our successes, failures, triumphs and tribulations, our social status, our careers, our relationships...

Let's look at one of these, the body, for it can serve as an instructive metaphor, illustrating just how arbitrary and deeply conditioned the process of identification is.

We've come to delineate certain portions of the body (fingers, toes, organs, joints, tissues, cells) as separate objects. However, the body is actually *one* indivisible thing, is it not? The body doesn't *have* separate parts but is an entire whole. For example, take the part of the body we designate as the "wrist." Where does that portion end and the rest of what we conventionally label "arm" begin? And where does the arm end and what we refer to as the "shoulder" begin? We of course understand that these designated parts are connected to the entirety of the body. However, our tendency is to conceive of them as having their own individual integrity and autonomous existence, as if they were somehow separable from the whole.

Now just as we do with the body and its seemingly separate parts, we divide the field of experience (what we might call the "body" of experience) into seemingly separate things. We call the separate parts of experience by many names—thoughts, memories, perceptions, feelings, sensations, and so on. However, these designated parts are not actually divisible from the entire body of experiencing itself. Conventionally, we of course make such distinctions, identifying the different portions of the body of experience as separate experiential phenomena. And yet, we cannot actually tell where the seemingly separate parts of experiencing end and the whole of the experiential field begins. Like the ocean and its ever-changing waves, the parts and the whole are ultimately inseparable.

Now let's return to the question of identity. The sense of who and what we are is in many respects a function of what parts of the "body of experiencing" we are focusing upon and in turn deeming as more or less significant. For example, there may be a focus on certain thoughts, emotional states, or personality characteristics and a corresponding sense of identification with those. At other times, the attentional focus may shift toward some other aspect or dimension of the "body of experiencing" such as our physical existence, gender, race, political affiliation, or maybe our favorite sports team. And when this attentional shift in emphasis occurs, a different sense of identity or self-sense becomes more predominant.

All of which raises a very provocative question: Exactly what part or parts of the full body of experiencing *are* we? Are we these physical bodies? Are we the myriad thought streams coursing through what we call "mind"? Or maybe we're the ever-changing cascade of energetic qualities and emotions being experienced? And what about all that we are seeing, hearing, touching, and tasting? Are we not also *those* parts of the "body of experiencing"? Why reduce or limit ourselves to just one part or parts? Wouldn't that be tantamount to looking at a finger or toe, a kidney or the brain, and imagining those somehow represent the whole of the body?

Isn't it somewhat arbitrary to claim we are only certain portions of the body of experiencing and not others? Feel that little flicker of energy in your stomach? Isn't that also what you are? See the clouds floating in the spacious blue of space? Maybe that's you too! Hear the sounds of crickets at night, feel that rush of love, the discomfort of uncertainty, the warmth of social connection? Maybe it is *all* you...

What Are We?

We often think of ourselves in quite fixed, limited, close-ended ways. The image we hold of ourselves is as a time- and space-bound creature, one that is identifiable by a particular concrete, localized, physical body that houses a recognizable and stable personality and mind.

But closer examination reveals something else altogether. For when we actually *feel* what is present here (rather than assuming that we know what it is), when we look at what is arising within the presumed boundaries of who and what we think of ourselves as, we discover that we are far more dynamic and ultimately indefinable than previously imagined. You can listen to a recording for this chapter at http://www.newharbinger.com /41818.

PRACTICE

Right now, look at what's arising experientially. Feel whatever is being felt. This must be who and what we are for after all, what else could we be other than what is being experienced? Look and feel what is presently happening; what is it that's being experienced?

In other words, what are you?

Just look at your experience right now, this vast symphony of sensations continually arising and then passing away, the multitude of energies that appear and then vanish in a flash, this kaleidoscope of flickering thoughts and feelings, here for an instant and then gone, an infinite array of experiential textures and qualities bursting forth and then disappearing, just like that...

Could it be that *all* of that is what you are?

Ask yourself if this matches the conventional notions you may hold about yourself as a fixed, solid, bounded creature.

Look at what's here and you may discover that you are not in fact fixed but are forever on the move, always shifting, always being reshaped.

Maybe what you are is this ever-flowing, ever-fluctuating dynamism that has no discernible edge or boundary to it, a ceaseless, unpredictable explosion of life that never holds still for even a second.

Could it be that what you are is quite literally beyond any definition or classification? Maybe the best we can say about ourselves is that we are cosmic shape-shifters, never resolving as any one thing but only ever a universe of inconceivable, indescribable qualities and characteristics, like a thousand million flavors being tasted each instant.

The Impossibility of Measurement

Even our most sophisticated tools of scientific measurement can only ever *approximate* the qualities and characteristics of things. To be sure, some tools are more accurate than others. A thermometer that is broken will be far less capable of capturing our "true" temperature than one that is well calibrated. Now, let's say we have a very accurate, high-tech digital thermometer and it indicates that my temperature is 98.6 degrees, exactly midway between 98.5 and 98.7. However, suppose we locate an even more precise thermometer and it reveals my actual temperature to be 98.59 degrees. Not quite 98.60, but very close. From the standpoint of wanting to determine with greater precision what my actual body temperature is, that's great. However, what if we develop an even *more* sophisticated measuring device and, lo and behold, discover that my temperature is actually 98.589. Not quite 98.590. But again, very, very close.

The point of this example is to highlight that no matter how precise our measurement tools may be, we will never be able to determine with absolute certainty the true quantity or size of anything because there are an infinite number of possible points between any two values. While it's possible to get close, the true measure of things is always just beyond our reach. In other words, the qualities and characteristics of things are indeterminate. And in the same way that we cannot precisely measure the quantitative dimensions of material objects, it is also not possible to determine the exact nature of qualitative, subjective phenomena. Let's look at the familiar state of mind we call "anxiety."

PRACTICE

Imagine a horizontal line, starting at "0." Moving right, the numbers go up, +1, +2, +3, and so on with each number on the line representing one "unit of anxiety." Now, pretend that a feeling described as "non-anxious" or calm falls at "0" on our imaginary line. As we move forward, we begin to head in the direction of feeling less calm and more anxious.

Now, let us suppose that +1 on our number line represents a state we would characterize as no longer calm, but "anxious." By the time we get to +2, we're feeling intensely anxious and at +3, we start to experience a panic attack.

But here's the question: Is there an actual point where it can be determined that we have now left one state and entered another? At what exact place along our number line do we clearly move from one way of characterizing reality (calm) to a different one (anxious)? If we say that once we get to +1, we've now fully arrived at the state we can label as anxiety (and can no longer be considered calm), are we saying that at 0.99 on our line we haven't quite moved fully into the anxious state?

Well, one might counter by saying, "okay, at 0.99 we're starting to feel the faint rumblings of anxiety even if it hasn't taken complete hold of us yet." *Starting* to feel? What exactly does that mean? Can we not get more precise about this? Imagining the line as representing increasing degrees of anxiety, are we saying that it is exactly at 0.99 that the first murmurings of what we might call anxiety have begun to emerge? What about 0.98999999? Were there any faint hints of anxiety at that point?

If we imagine moving experientially from a relative state of calm to one we would describe as lacking in calmness or anxious, the question I'm posing here is, at what exact point on the line do we consider that we have definitively left the land of calm and entered a new territory characterized by a lack of calm? Can we clearly identify exactly at what point calmness has ended and anxiety begun? No!

The reality is that whether we're talking introspectively or mathematically, we are not able to determine precisely when a given state of mind ends and another presumably begins since there are, as in the above example of measuring temperature, an infinite number of possible points between any ending and subsequent starting point.

The point of all of this is to illustrate that just as it is not really possible to determine the measure of something arguably more concrete such as body temperature, so too is it impossible to say definitively that we are now abiding in one state such as anxiety and not another. For if we see subjective states of mind as dynamic, which they clearly are, and therefore as existing on some sort of continuum illustrated by our imaginary number line, then we're faced with the same impossibility of determining when a given state has actually ended and another begun.

We can never pin down the precise beginning, middle, or end of *any* experiential state. And this is just as true subjectively as it is neurologically, hormonally, or mathematically.

So what does this mean, practically speaking?

Well, just look at the immediacy of your present moment experience—no matter how you might attempt to describe what it is, the actual beginning of that experience cannot be found or determined. In reality, separate or discrete states of mind are an abstraction because everything exists as a seamless continuum.

Many Flavors, One Taste

Experiences, no matter their distinctive nature, share several things in common. First, experiences are present. Second, they are known. Third, they are by nature dynamic and unstable. And fourth, they cannot be definitively described or characterized conceptually.

Experiential moments described as "clear," while obviously distinct qualitatively from those moments characterized as "confused," are at the same time equal in that they are both present and known, they are both impermanent, and they both contain infinite experiential depth; that is, they cannot be pinned down as being one (de)finite thing. Every experience has its distinctive flavor—no question. But the fact of its presence, the fact that it is here, that is the one taste, the taste of everything.

While we can certainly practice various techniques to move from one experience interpreted as unaware or unenlightened to another labeled as more aware, more mindful, or more enlightened, there is another choice...

PRACTICE

Notice right now that experience, regardless of its label, is always present. That is its fundamental nature: to be present, to be here, effortlessly. All experiences, no matter how they may be described, are present.

And so presence need not be cultivated or developed. Presence—the hereness of all experiential moments—is already the case. It is inescapable. A moment characterized as not being aware or mindful is just as here, just as present as a moment described as being fully awake and mindful. You see?

From this experiential vantage, what we call clarity is equal to confusion; mindlessness is equal to mindfulness; nonrecognition of awareness is equal to recognition of awareness; believing we are a psychological self is equal to seeing through that self-identification, not in terms of the different flavors and textures of such experiences but in terms of their presence.

Right now, as you sit here, see that all experiences arise and pass away, and while they are distinct from one another, they are at the same time equal in their existence, impermanence, and indescribability.

And so, you can relax; reality is already here, and presence is already present. A moment of boredom or excitement, of sorrow or joy, it is all the ultimately uncharacterizable presence of experiencing.

I invite you to feel the equalness of everything, the non-difference in all experience even as you savor the lusciousness of all its distinctive flavors.

Experience Doesn't Matter

Here's a radical proposition—*what you are experiencing doesn't actually matter*. Of course, such a notion runs counter to just about everything we've ever been taught or conditioned to believe. It's pretty much a foregone conclusion that we should try to secure certain types of experiences we've come to define as "positive," while avoiding those we consider to be "negative." And so to suggest otherwise may seem quite crazy, preposterous even… But let's just experiment with this for a few moments, the possibility that it doesn't actually matter what we're experiencing. You can listen to a recording of the following practice at http://www.newharbinger.com/41818.

PRACTICE

Simply allow yourself to consider that it matters not what the particular qualities or characteristics are that you're feeling.

Consider that your experience need not be one iota different than it is, that it's completely perfect, exactly as it is, that nothing about it is wrong or out of place or lacking in any way whatsoever.

In fact, see that it is not even possible for you to be experiencing anything *other* than what is presently being felt, seen, sensed, or heard.

Feel the profundity of this, that reality cannot be any other way than the way it is…until it is…

Consider the possibility that no experience matters more or less than any other for they are all present, all wildly alive.

For these next few moments, see what it is like to let everything be fine, to let each and every experience be okay, to allow every thought, every feeling, every sensation to be the unavoidable, perfectly miraculous, inconceivable expression of life that it is.

The Magic Show

In many if not most teachings (including, ironically, those described as "non-dual"), the message is, more often than not, portrayed in terms of opposed frameworks—self vs. no-self, freedom vs. bondage, limitation vs. unboundedness, conceptuality vs. non-conceptuality, and so on. However, while framing things in these terms may have some utility and value, our direct experience encompasses both sides of the seeming dualistic divide they suggest.

PRACTICE

A sense of being an individual, a person, a unique self separate from other unique selves is unquestionably something that we have all experienced. There is no denying the felt sense of individuality, the feeling of being a subject encountering a world of other seeming subjects and objects.

And yet, see right now if you can actually find this seemingly substantial thing you call "the self." Yes, there can be a sense of being bound by these bodily skin suits. And yet look to see if any clear boundaries can actually be found, any concrete divisions separating self from other.

In whatever locale we imagine the separate, psychological self to exist, all that we find there is a dynamic flow of thoughts, feelings, sensations, and memories. And even those elements we say constitute the self cannot themselves be found to exist either, at least not as bounded, clearly identifiable, discrete "things."

After all, ask yourself, what is a thought? A feeling? A sensation? It can't really be said, can it?

So, we experience the sense of being a separate, unique individual. And yet, when we look for them, neither the phenomenon of self nor the sense of separation it implies can be found. I call it the magic show of phenomena—things appear to exist, and from one vantage do. And yet they cannot actually be found when looked for. Experiential phenomena are here and at the same time *not* here. I guess the fairest thing we can say is that phenomena, including the self, neither exist nor don't exist. In other words, the world is non-dual, "not-two."

To the dualistically-inclined conceptual mind, the idea that there is both the presence and absence of a self appears to be an unresolvable contradiction. And yet it is precisely our experience. We seem to exist as separate selves, but no such self can be found to exist. Here but not here, existence and nonexistence co-occurring.

It's the same with the myriad states of mind experienced—fear, joy, sorrow, bliss—like rainbows, they appear with great vividness but when looked for, cannot be found, at least not as we imagined.

Think of the self like a point in the sky—a distinct localization of experiencing but at the same time, indivisible from the rest of the sky. Unique waves…yet simultaneously, the vast and boundless sea.

Everything Is What You Want

Think for a moment about something you are aspiring to realize in your life. What, for example, are you hoping to get from reading this book? Whatever that may be—a greater sense of freedom, love, happiness, openness, compassion, harmony, ease—it matters not. For these next few moments, let yourself imagine that *every single experience* is actually a perfect expression of whatever it is you are aspiring to realize.

PRACTICE

Let's say it's a sense of freedom you are seeking.

With eyes opened or closed, just consider the possibility that every momentary thought, every feeling, every sensation, every memory and visual image that might appear is in fact nothing other than freedom. What does this freedom you are seeking look like?

Well, it looks like *whatever* is happening in experience! Regardless of any beliefs you may be harboring about how freedom should, in theory look, for now, let it look exactly like *this*.

Allow this freedom to be inclusive of everything. See every experience as the very freedom you've been searching for. Let it be that radical.

From this vantage, realize that there can be no entering or exiting the vast, radically all-inclusive, all-embracing nature of this freedom you've been seeking for there is *only* this, *only* this vast open-endedness, this great freedom that moves as all things, dances as all things, shapes itself into all things…

See that there is no place to arrive, no state to enter into, no particular experience to achieve to realize this freedom, for freedom is every place, every state, every experience.

The Indescribability of Everything

Traditions speak about the discovery of *one taste*, the realization that all phenomena, all experiences are different versions or expressions of a singular, undivided reality. But how, you might ask, could life have "one taste" when everything has its own obviously unique and distinctive flavor? How can one claim that the experience of, say, happiness has the same "taste" as a state such as sorrow or anger? How can we say something soft "tastes" or feels the same as something hard or rough? How can sorrow have the same taste as joy, or pain the same taste as pleasure? While qualitatively, these clearly represent *very* different textures or flavors of experience, the single, one taste of everything is realized by discovering what all experiences have in common. You can download a recording for this chapter at http://www.newharbinger.com/41818.

PRACTICE

For the next few moments, cup your hands together very gently. Just feel the sensations that are present as your two hands make contact with one another. Feel into the innumerable energetic qualities and characteristics that are showing up.

Now notice how impossible it is to characterize this.

Clearly there is experience occurring. But there is simply too much information, too many details, too much richness and subtlety to be able to place the experience in any kind of neat and tidy category or description. This simple experience of feeling the contact between your hands is quite literally beyond words, beyond concepts. You could spend a whole lifetime trying to put what's present into words, but you would never succeed. It's simply not possible.

Now, remaining in this position, squeeze your hands together tightly. Feel how distinct the feelings and sensations are now compared to what was being experienced a few moments ago when the hands were just lightly touching one another. But just as you found previously, notice how the complexity and density of information cascading through consciousness as you grasp the hands together more tightly is again not describable. As before, the experience is literally beyond description.

While these two experiences clearly have their own distinctive and identifiable flavors or signatures, at the same time they share a common "taste" and that is their ultimately indefinable nature. And this turns out to be the case with *every* experience. Happiness, sadness, cold, warmth, sorrow, elation...all different in their descriptions yet identical in their inconceivability.

Feel this, the single, indescribable taste of everything.

It's Exactly What You Think It Is...
and So Much More

Throughout this book, I have been saying in as many ways as I can that our conventional descriptions of things fail to capture their inconceivable depth and complexity. However, at the same time that experiences are not what we imagine or conceive of them to be, we could also say that things are *exactly* what we say or think they are. Of course, it sounds like I am contradicting myself. So, let me explain...

What we call "fear" is exactly that. It's not sadness. It's not anger. It's not joy. It's fear! That descriptive label is indicative of *something*. If I tell you that I am afraid, something about what is appearing experientially is being conveyed to you. Similarly, if I say to you, "Look at how beautiful the clouds are today," those words direct your attention to notice those curious white puffy objects in the sky and not the bright yellow orb nearby.

In other words, a cloud is exactly what I say it is. It's not a dog or a mountain or a sunset. It's a cloud! As with fear, we could say that clouds have their own distinctive textural quality. Everything has its own unique signature that makes it what it is and enables consciousness to characterize it through the medium of concepts and language. The mind's capacity to discriminate one thing or experience from another is truly remarkable. But how are we even able to do that? How, in less than a nanosecond, can we see or hear something, and then seemingly recognize what that object or experience is? It is absolutely mind-boggling just how this magical process of object recognition and description occurs, without one scintilla of seeming effort or intention.

Look outside your window at something, say a tree. The knowledge of what that particular object is seems as if it is present, almost before we even look. The seeing and the conceptualization of whatever is being seen appear to arise together. Now imagine standing on a high ledge, overlooking the sea hundreds of feet below and suddenly finding yourself visited by that familiar experiential pattern we call *fear*. Again, the label seems to arrive coincident with the experience.

So yes, the experience we call fear is very precisely what we say it is. It's fear! But, even though we have this extraordinary capacity to render experience conceptually and linguistically, we cannot actually pin down what our descriptive labels are in fact referring to. Yes, fear is fear and we *know* that it is fear (as opposed to some other state). And yet, we cannot really get to the bottom of what fear or any other experience actually is. Our ideas, however indicative they may be, are simply not capable of capturing the seemingly infinite, bottomless nature of experience.

It's all quite paradoxical. We can say what things are; we can seemingly distinguish this from that and communicate that knowledge of what a thing or experience is, whether to ourselves or others. And yet, when we investigate what our words and concepts are actually pointing to, we find that the experiences themselves contain so much more depth, complexity, and nuance than our interpretations would otherwise suggest. So yes, our experiences are exactly what we say they are and at the same time, so much more than that…

Epilogue: *This Life That Is Also Death*

On a Saturday in October of 2015, my mom, who had been valiantly battling pancreatic cancer for almost two years, took a turn for the worse. It was clear to all of us that day that she wouldn't be with us for much longer. Sunday was a very rough day for her. But on Monday, she seemed to rally. So, I decided to head back to my home in Northern California knowing that I would return in a couple of days' time but also concerned that she might not live that long. I had the sense when we said what was the sweetest of goodbyes to one another that it might be the last time I ever saw her again.

Sure enough, no sooner had I returned home that night than she became very, very ill again. The next morning my brother texted me saying that he thought Mom was dying—possibly in the next hour or so. So, I began the six-hour trek back to Los Angeles.

When I arrived, she was somehow miraculously still with us. I walked into my parents' bedroom and my dear dad, who had been so tenderly holding her hand for hours, said he wanted to give me the gift of holding it myself for a few minutes. It was quite something to be there in those moments as she took those long, slow breaths, very clearly beginning to make that mysterious transition to what we call death.

Fifteen or so minutes later, my dad returned to take her hand and I then sat at the edge of the bed, gently rubbing her feet, together with my brother, sister-in-law, daughter, and niece, all with their hands on her as well. As we sat there, I found myself whispering silently to her that it was fine for her to let go, to surrender into great peace and that we would all, especially Dad, be fine. It was very powerful. I could sense the swirl of emotions in the room, the rush of complex feelings and thoughts running through each of us: sons losing their mom, a husband losing his beloved, granddaughters losing their remarkable grandmother... The dramatic nature of it all was quite something—very palpable, gritty, and real.

As we were gathered together, feeling our dear Lena's life slipping away and the immensity of responses we were each having to that inevitability, I remembered that beyond all the stories and narratives any of us might be running about what was being experienced (none of which could ever possibly capture the infinite, inconceivable nature of it), there was just this simple naked presence of *what is*, extraordinary and at the same time, the simplest, most ordinary thing. Buddhism refers to it as "suchness," the sheer existence or beingness of everything. I found myself just relaxing into that. It was so obvious, so simple, and so real. No abstraction, but simple, pure actuality, pure presence, pure unelaborated experience.

As I sat in the naked simplicity of what was being experienced, I could feel my dear mom's breathing becoming slower and slower, her death feeling very imminent. (Mind you, all that I'm describing here really transpired in a matter of seconds.) Then, in a flash instant, that naked, raw, indescribable yet very tangible presence of reality seemed to grow brighter. And in the very instant of recognizing that simple, unadorned presence of what is, and feeling the power yet ordinariness of it, there was no more breath. My mother had passed...

It's impossible to really describe that moment. There were, of course, the very strong currents of emotion—in a flash this beautiful soul I so loved was gone. At the same time, her passing felt like a direct confirmation from her of the inconceivable nature of everything including what we call death, a potent reminder of the liberating power of moment-to-moment experience unencumbered by all the necessarily limited ways we define and interpret it. It felt that my sweet mom's passing was reminding me of what she and everything ultimately is—an indescribable, uncharacterizable actuality, this vast, mysterious presence that neither birth nor death can define for it transcends all categories, all descriptions, all definitions.

Postscript

Nothing I have said here is the absolute truth, for as I've been saying throughout these pages, and in as many ways as possible, it's simply not possible to convey in words or concepts what experience actually is, even as the immense power of language and conceptualization leads us to believe that we somehow can.

And since the reality of experience cannot be collapsed into any descriptive, interpretive framework, the best I could ever hope for is that through these words and concepts, I've been able to evoke *something* of the ultimately inconceivable, mysterious, open-ended nature of this great, unfathomable reality we call life.

Acknowledgments

I offer this book in gratitude to *all* my teachers and to the inconceivable mystery and intelligence that makes all teachings and things possible.

References

Klemm, W. R. 2011. "Neural Representations of the Sense of Self." *Advances in Cognitive Psychology* 7: 16–30.

The Enneagram Institute. 2017. "The Enneagram Institute." https://www .enneagraminstitute.com/.

The Myers & Briggs Foundation. 2018. "MBTI." http://www.myersbriggs .org/.

Walton, A. 2015. "7 Ways Meditation Can Actually Change the Brain." *Forbes.*

John Astin, PhD, is a songwriter, recording artist, spiritual teacher, and adjunct professor of psychology at Santa Clara University and Notre Dame de Namur University. He is author of *Too Intimate for Words*, *This Is Always Enough*, and *Searching for Rain in a Monsoon*.

Foreword writer **Adyashanti** is an American-born spiritual teacher devoted to serving the awakening of all beings. His teachings are an open invitation to stop, inquire, and recognize what is true and liberating at the core of all existence. Adyashanti is author of *The Way of Liberation*, *Falling into Grace*, *Emptiness Dancing*, *True Meditation*, and *The End of Your World*.

MORE BOOKS for the SPIRITUAL SEEKER

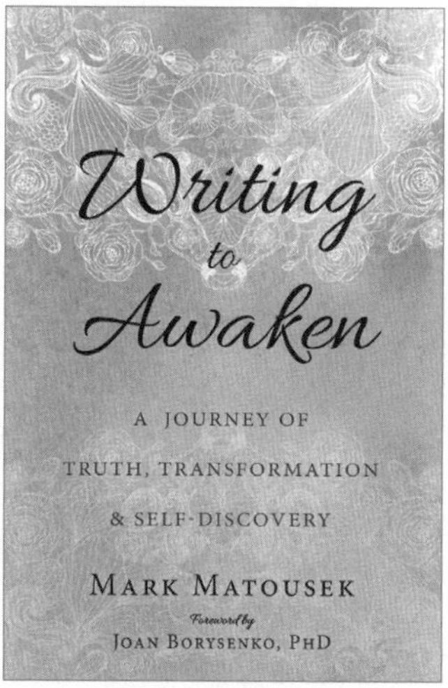

ISBN: 978-1626258686 | US $16.95

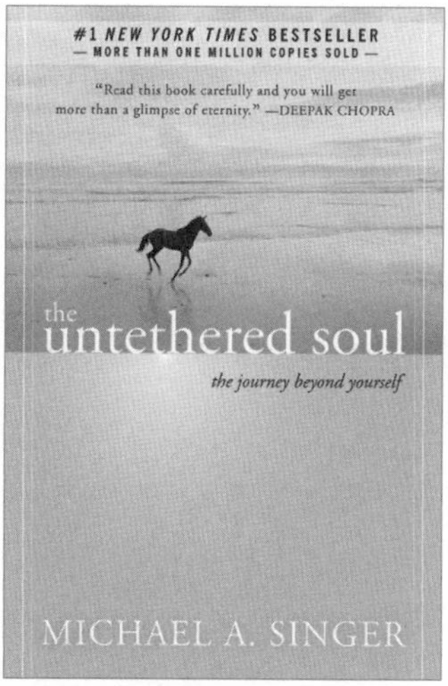

ISBN: 978-1572245372 | US $16.95

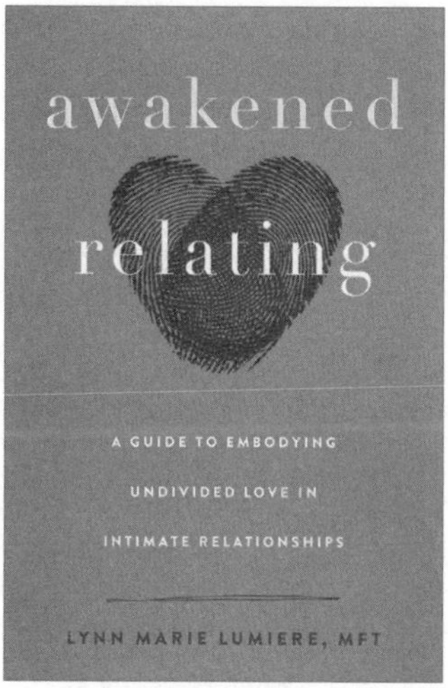

ISBN: 978-1684031016 | US $16.95

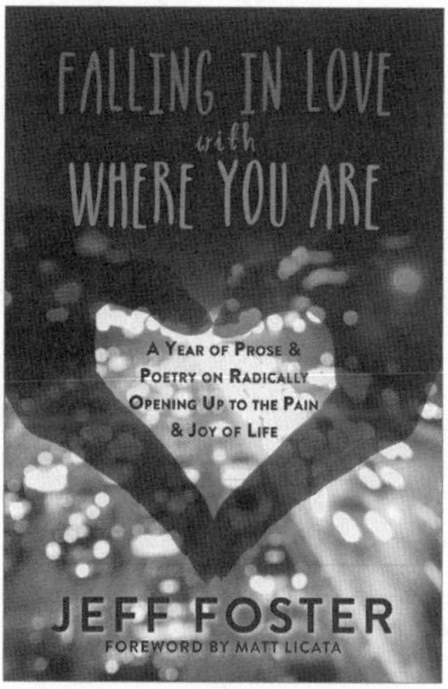

ISBN: 978-1626256415 | US $16.95

newharbingerpublications

NON-DUALITY PRESS | REVEAL PRESS

Sign up *for* our spirituality e-newsletter:

newharbinger.com/join-us

Register your **new harbinger** titles for additional benefits!

When you register your **new harbinger** title—purchased in any format, from any source—you get access to benefits like the following:

- Downloadable accessories like printable worksheets and extra content

- Instructional videos and audio files

- Information about updates, corrections, and new editions

Not every title has accessories, but we're adding new material all the time.

Access free accessories in 3 easy steps:

1. Sign in at NewHarbinger.com (or **register** to create an account).

2. Click on **register a book**. Search for your title and click the **register** button when it appears.

3. Click on the **book cover or title** to go to its details page. Click on **accessories** to view and access files.

That's all there is to it!

If you need help, visit:

NewHarbinger.com/accessories

new harbinger
CELEBRATING
4O YEARS